SEASONAL WORSHIP
FROM THE COUNTRYSIDE

Commendations for *Seasonal Worship from the Countryside*:

'During the last 20 years the countryside has passed through a time of unprecedented change. Many of the rural issues now are very different from those of the 1980s and 1990s, as indeed are the needs and aspirations of many now living in the country. The rural economy as a whole, and farming in particular, suffered immeasurable loss as a result of foot-and-mouth disease. Concerns such as rural service provision, countryside access and sustainability all now feature on the national political agenda.

'Yet at the heart of most rural communities there is still the Church, where all these issues continue to be brought together in worship and prayer, as well as in the wider life of practical, prophetic and pastoral ministry.

'I am sure that this book will not only be the much needed replacement for the Arthur Rank Centre publication *Church Services for the Farming Year*, now 14 years old, but will also prove to be an invaluable means of resourcing the ministry and mission of the rural Church in this century. I commend it to you and also pay tribute to the effort and expertise of its authors. The book is an expression of their faith and vision and their understanding of life in the countryside. I pray it will help many to offer their worship to the God who, whilst making all things new, transcends all change.'

Revd Dr Gordon Gatward, Director of the Arthur Rank Centre,
Royal Agricultural Society of England, Stoneleigh, Warwickshire

'In an original and imaginative synthesis of ancient rural traditions and contemporary Christian spirituality, this book offers a rich treasury of liturgical resources that will be welcomed by Christians in town and country alike. The Staffordshire Seven draw out the seams of seasonal celebration that are embedded in the very soil beneath our feet and make them delightfully accessible to all who long for rightful reconnection with all creation.'

Margaret Silf, Roman Catholic author and retreat conductor

'This book is the fruit of a partnership having depth and originality, identifying important issues and allowing a spiritual dialogue to take place in the context of worship. To encourage the rural Church to think in new ways and to develop services that are stimulating and imaginative, this book links together numerous passages, both the practical and the lyrical.

'The rural Church is finally being provided with resource material for worship and reflection through this work. It will fill a significant gap on the bookshelf of those concerned with worship in their communities. It also reminds us of our frailty and the need for continued reverence for both Creator and creation. This is a thoughtful and relevant publication which I highly commend to you. Thank you, Staffordshire Seven!'

Revd Patricia E. Pinkerton, Diocese of Gloucester

Seasonal Worship from the Countryside

The Staffordshire Seven

Published in Great Britain in 2003 by
Society for Promoting Christian Knowledge
Holy Trinity Church
Marylebone Road
London NW1 4DU

Acknowledgements for the use of copyright material reproduced in this book
can be found on pp. 233–9.

British Library Cataloguing-in-Publication Data
A catalogue record for this book is available from the British Library

ISBN 0-281-05446-0

10 9 8 7 6 5 4 3 2 1

Designed and typeset by Kenneth Burnley, Wirral, Cheshire
Printed in Great Britain by Clays, Bungay, Suffolk

Contents

AUTUMN

COMMUNITY OCCASIONS

TIMES OF TRAGEDY AND LOSS

About the Authors

The Staffordshire Seven

Michael Ayden
Michael Ayden trained for the ordained ministry in the Methodist
Church at Nottingham University (the East Midlands Ministerial
Training Course), where the subject of his dissertation was 'What
future for the Church in rural areas?' He subsequently lived for
over 20 years in the Peak District National Park, in pastoral
charge of four rural churches in north Staffordshire. In 2000 he
retired and now acts as a non-supernumerary minister in east
Suffolk. He is a member of Christian Rural Concern and the
Rural Theology Association.

Tony Hodgson
Tony Hodgson was brought up in rural Hampshire. Until his
retirement in 2000 he worked for 30 years in Anglican ministry in
small communities in Huntingdonshire and Staffordshire. During
this time, he refounded the Little Gidding Community and
subsequently co-founded the Rural Theology Association and
Christian Rural Concern. He now lives with his wife Judith in
Berwick-upon-Tweed in north Northumberland. He is the author
of *Country People, an Endangered Species*.

Nicky Hoskin-Stone
Nicky Hoskin-Stone studied Divinity in Liverpool and Lancaster,
followed by a Master's Degree in Educational Psychology which
researched pupil concepts of God in world faiths. She is currently
Head of Religious Education and Co-ordinator of Personal Social
and Health Education in a Derbyshire secondary school. She is a
member of the Society of Friends and represents them on the
Derbyshire Standing Advisory Council for Religious Education.
Nicky's varied interests include membership of the Chesterfield
Garland Clog Team, and Feet First Appalachian Dance Team.
Nicky and her husband, Leon, live in Chesterfield.

John Lovatt

John Lovatt comes from an old north Staffordshire family. For many years he ran the family ceramic business together with his brother and for 11 of those years also farmed in a small way; at present he spends most of his time involved in organizations dedicated to relating the Christian faith to daily work, and restoring a sixteenth-century farmhouse.

Noël Lovatt

Born and bred in London, Noël Lovatt has lived very happily since 1963 in north Staffordshire. In 1971 she, her husband and three children moved to a small farm, overlooking the valley where the River Trent rises. She helped her husband to look after a dairy herd and young stock, then ran a livery yard, and she now assists in her daughter's horse-riding and training centre. In 1973, John and Noël both became life-professed members of the Third Order of the Society of St Francis. They attend their local parish church.

Linda J. Probyn

Linda J. Probyn is a licensed lay minister/prayer guide with a special interest in the spiritual development of both individuals and communities. She has lived in the country all her life and for many years ran an animal rescue shelter. She is a member of the Order of Aidan and Hilda and the Association of Creation Spirituality. She has a special interest in meditation and creative imagination in prayer, the Celtic tradition, and native/indigenous and tribal spiritual traditions from around the world. She has three grown-up children and now shares her home with a border collie, a tabby cat and various guests.

John Whitehead

John Whitehead, who has recently retired to Nantwich, served as a rural parish priest in Betley and Keele. Having been involved in the group from the beginning, he found that some memorable Rogation Walks and a genuinely communal celebration of the Millennium helped to create an even greater enthusiasm for *Seasonal Worship*. John was senior editor of *Rural Theology* until 2002 and currently tutors students for Christian Rural Concern. He and his wife Barbara have two daughters.

Foreword

For those of us who live and work in the country, and for anyone who enjoys leisure pursuits among the hills and valleys of Britain, the seasons play an important part in our lives. The intensity of light and length of day, the changing patterns of countryside, the variety of wildlife and the sheer beauty of nature remind us of the absolute generosity of our Creator God.

BSE and foot-and-mouth disease were devastating for many farmers and rural businesses. Life has changed in the country-side – probably for ever. In the midst of this upheaval, creation has continued in profusion, reminding us that stewardship of the earth is God-given.

This publication is timely. It is intended for ecumenical and community use, and the material offered can be adapted as appropriate. Children and young people are often to be found within our rural worship and the material here offers the whole Christian Church the opportunity to focus on the rhythm of the cycle of life in relation to the land, work and living of the countryside. Through the background information, it facilitates worship for those who are slightly removed from the rural scene.

Wherever we live and work and have our being, our daily food is something for which to be profoundly grateful. In a world of changing values, it is good to be able to remember the production and processes that bring food to the world's table within the context of the Christian calendar.

This book brings affirmation to those who worship and work in the countryside. May it sow seeds and in due season bear fruit for those who worship with it.

ROSEMARY WASS

Rosemary Wass is a former vice-president of the British Methodist Conference and a well-known speaker and preacher. She is partner with her husband on a 193-acre organic farm in Yorkshire.

Acknowledgements

This book is the result of collaboration and participation by many people – not only the Staffordshire Seven themselves but also those who have supported them.

First, we would like to thank the Arthur Rank Centre at Stoneleigh. The rural church officers at the Centre – the Revd Dr Gordon Gatward, Canon Jeremy Martineau and Mrs Jenny Carpenter – encouraged us to go ahead in the first place. Later they carefully sifted through the draft material, making many useful and constructive comments.

Second, we are grateful for the support of the Rural Theology Association (RTA) and Christian Rural Concern (CRUC). The President of CRUC, Bishop Alan Chesters, provided helpful suggestions at an early stage and both organizations offered help as the book took shape. The journal of the RTA, *Rural Theology*, publicized our work, resulting in many helpful contacts. We also received valuable publicity in the magazine *Country Way*. A meeting of *Praxis* in June 2000 led to further widespread interest in the project.

Next, we would like to thank all those who field-tested our material. Twenty-six people, both lay and ordained, formed our panel of field-testers. As well as finding their comments helpful, we were immensely heartened by the enthusiasm they showed for the project. A number of field-testers also offered their own material. Due to the amount of material generated through the years, space has been found for only a few of these.

Last but not least, we are deeply indebted to the Editorial Director at SPCK, Joanna Moriarty, who fairly brimmed with enthusiasm as soon as she heard of *Seasonal Worship*. She and her SPCK colleagues have entered most co-operatively and sympathetically into the process of preparing it for publication. We have greatly appreciated their support and professional guidance.

Abbreviations for Hymn Books and Bibles

Bibles

AV   Authorized Version
NIV   New International Version
NRSV   New Revised Standard Version
REB   Revised English Bible
RSV   Revised Standard Version

Hymn books

CG   *Common Ground*
CP   *Come and Praise*
HO&N   *Hymns Old and New*
JP   *Junior Praise*
MP   *Mission Praise*
NEH   *New English Hymnal*
OB   *Oxford Book of Carols*

Introduction

This book came into being because of the marked absence of seasonal and other special services for rural situations. Field-testing of the worship material in different parts of the country brought an enthusiastic response, with requests for a full publication.

Seasonal Worship from the Countryside covers both the rural calendar and the Christian year, and also important events in the life of the community and the individual.

Furthermore, Christians who live in a city or town should not feel excluded, since many of the services can be used or adapted for a non-rural setting.

Suggestions for use

Most of the book consists of orders of service which can be taken straight off the page for worship. Many have introductions, providing historical and social background, suggestions for involving young people, and resources such as poems and practical preparations. A wide range of biblical verses and readings is included, but non-biblical readings are also offered in some places.

Collects and other prayers which are available in other books are usually referred to but not set out in full. The two widely used versions of the Lord's Prayer are given on page 227, together with one in use in New Zealand.

The Staffordshire Seven, the authors of this book, have brought to it a breadth of personal experience, from their lives in school, parish, district, farm and home. The book is the result of five years' work, underpinned by prayer and dialogue with a wide variety of Christian people. Their hope is that readers will discover in the following pages much more than a collection of services; rather a spiritual treasury for private, prayerful reflection as well as for gathered worship, enriching their lives as followers of the Christian Way.

WINTER

Advent

Background

The word 'Advent' means 'Arrival' and this season was traditionally seen as a time of preparation for the festival of Christmas. It was a time to reflect on the solemn themes of Heaven, Hell, Death and Judgement and to abstain from certain foods (particularly meat), and this is still the practice in some countries.

In the Middle Ages, there were five Sundays in Advent and this has perhaps survived in the Fifth Sunday before Christmas having its own traditional title of 'Stir-up Sunday' from the Collect Prayer for that day. It was thought to be the right time for making Christmas puddings.

Today

Advent had almost disappeared from our own culture but has made a comeback through Advent calendars and the Advent crown or wreath. However, the sense of its being a season of preparation and solemnity has probably gone for ever except among Christians.

Some Christian families use an Advent crown as a centrepiece for a special meal each weekend before Christmas, with candles or oil lamps providing the other illumination. If there are members of the family who enjoy singing or who play instruments, there can be singing after the meal, preferably *not* carols; if you look, there are plenty of hymns and songs suitable for this time of year.

Such rituals as lighting the candles on the Advent crown, having a special meal each weekend or decorating a Jesse Tree, help to make Advent more of a time for proper preparation for the coming of our Lord.

Christmas tree festival

In an age of large institutions where it is easy to feel that nothing can be achieved on a small scale, it is refreshing and inspiring to read what a small village in Warwickshire accomplished. Mrs Elisabeth Ashworth describes what happened:

'The idea of a Christmas Tree Festival came to me early in 2000 as a way our village could celebrate Jesus' millennium. Little did I realize how successful it would be, inspiring and enriching the village and our visitors to such an extent that it had to be extended by seven days after the original three, which were over the weekend before Advent Sunday.

'The response from our small village, with its 80 inhabitants, was overwhelming and the idea really gripped their imagination. Small groups and some individuals worked together to form their ideas. Those less sure of their artistic talents cut out and made various symbols. Others baked Christmas tree or star-shaped biscuits for the refreshments, or lent us their tree stands or white lights for each tree.

'The cost was kept low because someone kindly offered us trees of all sizes and shapes which wouldn't be of much use as normal Christmas trees. Publicity was done by putting up posters in the village and neighbouring villages, sending out a leaflet to all ministers within reach and by word of mouth.

'The festival started on the Friday and the church was open every day from 10 a.m. until 5 p.m. There were always three people in the church – one to welcome visitors, one to make tea and the other to wander around chatting to people as needed. A programme was provided with biblical references and details of the trees.

'The primary aim of the festival was to share our faith with others so admission and programmes were free, with 50 pence being charged for a cup of tea or coffee and home-made biscuit. To show that our faith is a living, loving faith going beyond our own community, money donated was given to an inner-city parish in Coventry to help with one of their community projects.

'On the same weekend, there was a concert on the Saturday evening and a Service of Advent Praise on the Sunday evening.'

The trees were as follows:

1. A small tree on the font, surrounded by lush greenery, symbolized the Garden of Eden.

2. Noah's tree was in a boat-shaped container, with the tree as the mast and animals made or collected by the Sunday School. There were also a dove and a rainbow.

3. Abraham and Isaac: at the base of the tree there was a coil of rope, a knife and an altar made of small stones; also stars, daggers, bundles of twigs and pictures of Abraham, and the ram caught in a thicket hung on the tree.

4. A ladder coming through the branches reached Gabriel in the heavens, with angels ascending and descending, as in Jacob's dream.

5. Joseph and his brothers were represented by different coloured ribbons each leading to a scroll bearing a name.

6. Plagues of locusts and bright green frogs adorned Moses' tree. Moses in the bullrushes appeared at the base. The manna from heaven was also represented.

7. Symbols for Jesse and Isaiah (quill pen and quotations) done in white and terracotta colours contrasted with the gold of David's tree.

8. David's tree had gold decorations, including a gold crown at the top.

9. Pure white roses and woodworking tools were used to illustrate Mary and Joseph.

10. John the Baptist's tree was surmounted by a dove representing the Holy Spirit, with blue ribbons for the River Jordan cascading down through it.

11. Two four-foot paper sculptures of Joseph and Mary with Jesus in her arms made a tableau set against the final tree, with the star of Bethlehem at the top.

To emphasize that the story of Jesus didn't stop with a baby in a manger, two crosses made out of Christmas tree trunks were also included: one for the cross and passion with a purple robe and crown of thorns (made out of brambles); the other, for the risen, ascended and glorified Christ, was sprayed gold all over and topped with a golden crown and golden rays.

There was also a Christmas tree in the porch with cut-outs of bells to celebrate the bell-ringing team, and a recording of bells was played.

Every hour, on the hour, the following prayer was said:

A Christmas prayer

> O God our Father,
> whose Word has come among us
> in the Holy Child of Bethlehem:
> may the light of faith illumine our hearts
> and shine in our words and deeds;
> through him who is Christ the Lord. **Amen.**

Poem

Advent 1955

The Advent wind begins to stir
With sea-like sounds in our Scotch Fir;
It's dark at breakfast, dark at tea,
And in between we only see
Clouds hurrying across the sky
And rain-wet roads the wind blows dry
And branches bending to the gale
Against great skies all silver-pale.

The world seems travelling into space,
And travelling at a faster pace
Than in the leisured summer weather
When we and it sit out together;
For now we feel the world spin round

On some momentous journey bound –
Journey to what? to whom? to where?
The Advent bells call out 'Prepare,
Your world is journeying to the birth
Of God made Man for us on earth'.

(John Betjeman, 1906–84)

Christmas

Background

Christmas Day is celebrated on 25 December, not because that is the date on which Jesus was born but because of the pre-Christian festival at the time of the winter solstice. Such a celebration featured in the Celtic, Anglo-Saxon and Roman calendars.
We may feel today that Christmas has again become mainly a pagan festival and that, as Christians, we are swimming against the tide at the beginning of the third Millennium. However, perhaps that is all the more reason to persevere in using our Christian rituals and celebrations.

Nowadays it also sometimes seems as though Christmas starts at the end of October and finishes on the evening of Christmas Day! Yet, for many centuries the Christian tradition has been that Christmas starts on Christmas Eve with Midnight Mass and carries on until the Feast of the Wise Men on 6 January, also known as Twelfth Night or Epiphany.

It is fashionable today to dream of a white Christmas, but up to the last century the colour associated with Christmas was green, because the greenery available at this time of the year was seen as a symbol of eternal life. Our ancestors used all sorts of greenery to decorate house and church, including holly which was thought to bring good luck to men, and ivy which was thought to do the same for women; often they were entwined to make garlands. It was supposed to be unlucky to bring greenery into the house before Christmas Eve; that was also the day when people went out to bring home the yule log, a large, slow-burning log, which was burnt to encourage the sun to return after the shortest day. Brands from the previous year's log were kept to ignite the new log.

One piece of greenery used in houses but never in churches was mistletoe, revered by the pagan Celts and Vikings for its supposedly magical properties. If enemies met under a tree bearing mistletoe, they would call a truce for the day. This may be the origin of the custom of kissing under the mistletoe – it was seen as a symbol of peace and friendship.

The association of the fir tree with Christmas is traced back to an English monk, St Boniface. He followed in the footsteps of St Columbanus and other Irish monks who initially spread the Christian message among the Frankish and Germanic tribes in the late sixth century. Boniface worked among the Germanic tribes in the eighth century. He found his converts worshipping the Sacred Oak of Thor so he chopped it down. A small fir tree was growing among the roots and he used it as a symbol of eternal life offered by the Christian religion. Decorated fir trees were found on the mainland of Europe long before they were introduced to this country, probably by Caroline of Brunswick, the wife of George IV, rather than by Prince Albert, the husband of Queen Victoria.

Carols were originally songs of joy, accompanying a dance (the word comes from the Italian 'carola', meaning a ring dance). Some carols, like the sixteenth-century 'Boar's Head Carol', are not religious. The Church took them up as part of popular culture. They were banned during the Reformation, and when they came back into use, tended to be confined to Christmas. Today, carols on a variety of Christian themes are being composed again.

The first Christmas crib was made by St Francis, using live animals. From that time, it became customary to display a crib scene in churches. Rather than straw, special herbs were used, known as cradle grasses or holy hay. These included rosemary and garden mint.

It has always been traditional to give a present to God's creatures at Christmas; this used to include a sheaf of corn fixed to the roof for the birds, and extra feed for animals. As St Francis said, on this day 'even the animals should share our joy'.

Play for children

This is suitable for a Christingle or Crib Service or school nativity play. The play also refers to Jesus's life and teaching. Biblical references are given on pages 12–13; they can be printed and given out at the end.

Cast: Mary, Joseph, three innkeepers and a number of children to take the other parts, each to have a suitable mask or clothing.

Start by singing 'Little donkey' (HO&N 859). The children can have bells, and wooden blocks to imitate the donkey's footsteps.

Mary and Joseph and the donkey start off at the back.

Mary   Is this Bethlehem at last, Joseph? I am very tired.

Donkey   I'm very tired too and my feet hurt.

Joseph   Yes, it's our journey's end. There are so many people around, I hope we can find suitable lodgings.

Mary   I feel my time is very near. We must find somewhere for me to have my baby.

They knock on a door.

Innkeeper 1   Are you looking for somewhere to stay? I'm afraid you'll have a lot of problems, with Bethlehem being so full. Try the inn at the other end of the town.

They walk a little way. A bird flies up to them.

Bird   If you want somewhere to have your baby, you can use my nest. It is high up and safe. No one will harm the baby and the wind in the branches will lull him to sleep.

Mary   Thank you, dear bird, but we'd find it difficult to fit into your nest and the baby might fall out. But I will remember and tell my son about you and he'll tell people that they should follow your example and trust in God.

They walk on a little and a sheep comes up to them.

Sheep	Why don't you come with me and I'll take you to my flock? There's a bright fire burning to keep you warm and my sisters will surround and protect you.
Joseph	Thank you, sister sheep, but we need some water to wash the baby and a cradle to put him in. But we will remember and tell our son about you and he'll tell stories about you and your sisters.

They pass by a tree and the tree bends down its branches to them.

Tree	There's a cave between my roots that's dry and sheltered and would keep the cold wind away from you and the baby. There'd be leafy branches for a bed and I'd stand guard over you.
Mary	Thank you, brother tree, but it wouldn't be suitable for me to have my baby so close to the road with people coming and going all the time. But I will remember and tell my son about you and one day you shall lift my son up and help him to make peace between God and all that's been created.

They go a little further.

Joseph	Here is another inn. Mary, you stay here with the donkey and I'll go and ask if they have any room.

Joseph knocks.

Innkeeper 2	It's no good expecting me to help you. The situation is quite impossible. It might be different if you looked clean and respectable and could afford to pay a lot.
Joseph	We're respectable people but tired and dirty after our journey. Can't you do anything for my wife? She's going into labour.
Innkeeper 2	That's all I need, a woman about to have a baby! Be off with you – try the poor place that calls itself an inn on the outskirts of the town.

They go a little further. A hen comes up to them.

Hen	I live in a nice little house with my chicks and you are welcome to come and share it with me. The cheeping of my chicks, as I spread out my wings over them, will

be a lullaby for your baby. I'll lay eggs for you to eat, if
you can find someone to cook them.

Mary   Thank you, dear mother hen, but I don't think we
can all fit into your house. But I will remember you
and tell my son about you. One day, he'll long to
protect Jerusalem in the same way as you gather your
chicks under your feathers.

A dog comes along the street.

Dog   My kennel is bigger than the henhouse and I'm sure I
could squeeze you and the baby in, though the
donkey'd have to stay outside. The baby could lie
between my paws and I would lick him and protect
him from all harm. When you return home, I'd follow
you and your son without looking back and be
faithful to him as my master until death.

Joseph   Thank you, brother dog, but I really don't think that
your kennel is big enough, although we'd like to have
your protection in this crowded town. And when we
leave Bethlehem, we'll take you with us to protect us
from any danger that might threaten our son.

Donkey   Dear master and mistress, I would gladly share my
stable with you if I had one, but at the moment I'm as
homeless as you.

Joseph   Yes, we're all in the same boat. We're very glad of the
way you have carried Mary so carefully and all the
work you do at home. One day, donkeys will have
their hour of glory when one carries our son into the
Holy City and all the people cry 'Hosanna'.

*By now, they should have arrived at the front of the church. They see the
third inn and Joseph knocks.*

Innkeeper 3 Goodness gracious me – don't tell me you're looking
for somewhere to stay, and your wife in that condition
as well. I'm at my wits' end with trying to fit people in.
I really can't offer you anything at all.

A cow puts her head over the door of her stable.

Cow   I can share my stable with you. There is straw on the floor and the baby can be put in my feed trough on some nice soft hay. I'll keep him warm with my breath and I can give milk for you to drink. There is room in my stable for your donkey as well so he can be safe and warm.

They all go in. The other animals, the innkeeepers and the tree gather round and everyone sings 'Away in a manger' (HO&N 776) or 'Joy to the world' (HO&N 370).

Biblical references behind the play

Often Christmas is seen in isolation from the rest of the Christian story. This play refers to future events in Jesus's life and teaching in the gospels.

Matthew 10.29–31 (NRSV): 'Are not two sparrows sold for a penny? Yet not one of them will fall to the ground unperceived by your Father . . . You are of more value than many sparrows.'

Luke 12.24 (NRSV): 'Consider the ravens: they neither sow nor reap, they have neither storehouse nor barn, and yet God feeds them. Of how much more value are you than the birds!'

Luke 15.3–7: Parable of the Lost Sheep.

John 10.11–16: Jesus is the Good Shepherd (see also the references in the Old Testament which Jesus would have known: Psalm 23, Isaiah 40.11, Ezekiel 34.1–16).

John 3.14–15 (REB): Jesus said: 'Just as Moses lifted up the serpent in the desert, so the Son of Man must be lifted up.' (The Old Testament reference here is to Numbers 21.6.)

Colossians 1.20 (NRSV): 'Through him [Jesus] God was pleased to reconcile to himself all things, whether on earth or in heaven, by making peace through the blood of his cross.'

Matthew 23.37 (NRSV): Jesus said: 'Jerusalem, Jerusalem, the city that kills the prophets and stones those who are sent to it! How often have I desired to gather your children together as a hen gathers her brood under her wings, and you were not willing!'

Luke 9.62 (NRSV): 'Jesus said to him, "No one who puts a hand to the plough and looks back is fit for the kingdom of God."'

Mark 14.27 (NRSV): 'Jesus said to them, "You will all become deserters; for it is written, 'I will strike the shepherd, and the sheep will be scattered.'"' (This comes in the Old Testament in Zechariah 13.7.)

Mark 14.46, 50 (NRSV): [The men] laid hands on [Jesus] and arrested him . . . All of them deserted him and fled.'

Zechariah 9.9–10 (NRSV): 'Rejoice greatly, O daughter Zion! Shout aloud, O daughter Jerusalem! Lo, your king comes to you . . . humble and riding on a donkey, on a colt, the foal of a donkey . . . He shall command peace to the nations.'

Matthew 21.1–11: Entry into Jerusalem.

Luke 2.7 (NRSV): [The baby] was laid in a manger, because there was no place for them in the inn.'

Street Nativity

This Christmas celebration is designed to involve the whole community, whether village or town. People of all ages can act out the Christmas story or participate by accompanying the characters to the different places.

Mary and Joseph's journey through Bethlehem would have taken place among noise and bustle. The shops and markets would be open and the craftsmen at work. So the Street Nativity should take place on Saturday morning or afternoon when the centre of the community is busy, with people shopping, etc. This should mean that the message of the Church and its important festival is brought out to the people.

The main characters of the story are: Mary, Joseph, donkey, innkeeper, Angel Gabriel, shepherds, wise men.

The story could start at a church or chapel with Mary and Joseph setting off on their journey. If possible, use a donkey: this adds excitement and interest for the children. Position the other characters at suitable places on the way, such as:

- the Angel Gabriel on top of a building with a flat roof;
- the shepherds in the local park;
- the wise men at the opposite corner of the park;
- the innkeeper at the local pub.

Shopkeepers should also be involved and bystanders follow the characters to the next stage of the story. The story can be expanded or reduced according to how great the community participation is. It is good to start in a simple way and expand further the following year. Prayers can be written to meet the needs of local people. Carols may be sung and the closing blessing given by a local minister at a pub.

Coffee and mince pies can be served at the church or chapel, or else the Nativity can end in a local club or community centre.

Many of the bystanders would not go to church even at Christmas but will receive the message of the birth of Jesus where they are. Children should be able to relate what they see to what they have been told in school, even if they have never been to church themselves.

This is one of the rare occasions when dressing up for an adult Nativity works. The colour and traditional robes add to the drama, particularly if you manage to get a donkey. It's also useful, if the street is crowded, for the actors to be easily recognized.

By the way, do remember to get permission from the local authority and police!

Activity for children

C - H - R - I - S - T - M - A - S

This is suitable for a service in school or at the beginning of a service in a church or chapel. Children make cards or placards with the letters of Christmas on the front and the sentence on the back so they can read them.

The children can wear costumes of some kind – they can be dressed as angels or wear tabards in suitable colours such as red and green. These could be made out of crêpe paper.

At the beginning of the service, the children walk up to the front with the minister or teacher and stand in a line facing those present. In turn, the children put up their letters and recite the appropriate sentence:

C is for **Christ**, our dear Lord and Saviour.

H is for **Holly** and for the **Hope** that Jesus brought.

R is for **Rejoicing** at this time of the year.

I is for **Indigestion** from eating too much!

S is for the bright **Star** that led the wise men to worship.

T is for **Tinsel** and **Turkey** and **Toys**.

M is for **Midnight** when animals kneel in reverence.

A is for **Angels** who sang sweetly in the sky.

S is for **'Silent night'** which we're going to sing now.

Everyone sings 'Silent night'.

Poems

Eddi's Service (AD 687)

Eddi, priest of St Wilfrid
In his chapel at Manhood End,
Ordered a midnight service
For such as cared to attend.

But the Saxons were keeping Christmas,
And the night was stormy as well.
Nobody came to the service
Though Eddi rang the bell.

'Wicked weather for walking,'
Said Eddi of Manhood End,
'But I must go on with the service
For such as care to attend.'

The altar-lamps were lighted,
An old marsh-donkey came,
Bold as a guest invited,
And stared at the guttering flame.

The storm beat on at the windows,
The water splashed on the floor,
And a wet, yoke-weary bullock
Pushed at the open door.

'How do I know what is greatest,
How do I know what is least?
That is my Father's business,'
Said Eddi, Wilfrid's priest;

'But three are gathered together,
Listen to me and attend.
I bring good news, my brethren!'
Said Eddi of Manhood End.

And he told the ox of a manger
And a stall of Bethlehem,
And he spoke to the ass of a Rider,
That rode to Jerusalem.

They steamed and dripped in the chancel,
They listened and never stirred,
While, just as though they were Bishops,
Eddi preached them the Word.

Till the gale blew off on the marshes
And the windows showed the day,
And the ox and the ass together
Wheeled and clattered away.

And when the Saxons mocked him,
Said Eddi of Manhood End,
'I dare not shut His chapel
On such as care to attend.'

(Rudyard Kipling, 1865–1936)

Christmas

Mass of Christ, Creation's Lord,
Marvels then were seen abroad:
In the heavens a star as guide
Voyaging through the cosmos wide;
While near the earth in wondrous guise,
Angelic hosts did fill the skies.
Shepherds rough, their sheep forsaking,
Came to find the young child waking;
Within a feed trough, in a stall
Lay on the straw the Lord of all.
Warm breath from ox, on guard the ass
That nothing harmful there should pass.
Our Lord, our God, did make them thus:
The animals, the world – and us.

(Noël Lovatt)

Christmas 1986

She calved on Christmas Day
A fine bull calf but she, we knew,
Was prone to milk fever, the disease
That robs the calved cow of calcium and of life.
Oft we had seen it, as searching through the fields
For one cow missing, we had found
The bulky body lying outstretched
While the calf stood dumbly by,
Uncertain in a world he did not know.
Quick, quick, plunge needle into shaking side,
The bottle held aloft
Lifegiving liquid pouring down the tube
Until she raised herself erect.
Ne'er a one had been lost,
But she was an old cow – what of her?
A new treatment had been given prior to calving
But still we wondered and felt doubt.
'I will sit up till midnight,' said our son
Then I took watch in silence until two.

My husband rose for milking – what was this?
Stretched out she lay and cold in four short hours.

Death at Christmas? Surely this is wrong,
Not in our thoughts and stories at this time?
But wait! We celebrate St Stephen's Day
And then the Holy Innocents,
Massacred to calm a tyrant's fear.
And with the Christ-child we can see
Foreshadowing of pain in Mary's heart
And death foreseen by gifts brought from afar.

With us that Christmas birth and death were mingled
As in our Christian life and thought and faith.

(Noël Lovatt)

The Oxen

Christmas Eve, and twelve of the clock.
'Now they are all on their knees,'
An elder said as we sat in a flock
By the embers in hearthside ease.

We pictured the meek mild creatures where
They dwelt in their strawy pen,
Nor did it occur to one of us there
To doubt they were kneeling then.

So fair a fancy few would weave
In these years! Yet, I feel,
If someone said on Christmas Eve,
'Come; see the oxen kneel,

In the lonely barton by yonder coomb
Our childhood used to know,'
I should go with him in the gloom,
Hoping it might be so.

(Thomas Hardy, 1840–1928)

Hymns

These Christmas hymns are especially suitable for a rural setting.

'In the bleak midwinter' (HO&N 326)
'Joy to the world' (HO&N 370)
'The holly and the ivy' (HO&N 645)

Plough Sunday

Background

This appears to be a very ancient festival, revived by the Victorians. Traditionally it is celebrated on the first Sunday after Epiphany, 6 January. Often the plough was fêted and drawn through the streets to be blessed in church. This was thought to ensure food for the coming year. The following day, Plough Monday, was the first day that work in the fields recommenced after Christmas.

When to use

Nowadays, with a good deal of ploughing taking place in the autumn, this service may be held on any appropriate Sunday which coincides with the start of the ploughing season or even during the week.

Preparation

A ploughshare, or some other part of the plough, is brought to the door, escorted by those who are to take a speaking part in the service and by other representatives of farming life. The leader (and choir) receive them at the door.

....

Welcome

A farmer or farm-worker   We come as representatives of our community to offer our work to the service of God.

Leader   We welcome you in the name of the One who made us all, people, animals and all the earth.

Hymn

'We plough the fields and scatter' (HO&N 719) *or*
'O Christ who holds the open gate' (page 26)

The leader (and choir) lead the way into the church or chapel,
followed by those carrying the ploughshare which is placed at the
front.

Verses from Psalm 104 (NIV, adapted)

Praise the Lord, O my soul.
O Lord my God, you are very great:
You are clothed with splendour and majesty,
wrapped in light as with a garment.
You make the clouds your chariot,
you ride on the wings of the wind.
You make winds your messengers,
flames of fire your ministers.
You make springs gush forth in the valleys;
they flow between the hills, giving drink to every creature.
You cause grass to grow for the cattle,
and plants for man to cultivate,
to bring forth food from the earth,
and wine to gladden the human heart,
oil to make the face shine,
and bread to strengthen the human heart.
The moon marks off the seasons,
and the sun knows when to go down.
You bring darkness, it becomes night,
and all the beasts of the forest come creeping out.
The sun rises, and they steal away;
they return and lie down in their dens.
Then people go out to their work,
to their labour until the evening time.
How many are your works, O Lord!
In wisdom you made them all;
I will sing praise to my God as long as I live.

or (based on Psalm 24, Genesis 8, Isaiah 28)

The earth is the Lord's:
And everything that is within it;
The wide extent of the world:
And all who live there.
The Lord looked upon the earth:
And filled it with blessings.
As long as the earth endures, seed time and harvest:
Summer and winter will never cease.
When farmers plough for planting, do they plough
continually?
Do they keep on breaking up and harrowing the soil?
When they have levelled the surface,
do they not plant wheat in its place and barley in its plot?
**Their God instructs them
and teaches them the right way.**

Prayer

O Creator God, who works through our hands and our minds,
as we strive to renew the face of the earth and bring your
kingdom; help us to feel reverence for the power you give us,
and to love the small part of your creation which you have
entrusted to each of us. **Amen.**

Our Acknowledgement of Sin

All kneel and a farmer's wife (*A*) and son or daughter (*B*) lead
the people:

A When we are ungrateful for the rain, sun and frost,
and forget they are God's gifts to us:
O God, forgive us.
B When we are blind to the mystery of germination,
and forget it is God's handiwork:
O God, forgive us.
A When we are careless with our beasts,
and forget they are God's creatures:
O God, forgive us.

B When we are unkind to those who work with us,
     and forget they are God's children:
     O God, forgive us.
A When we are careless about our work,
     and forget we are God's co-workers:
     O God, forgive us.
B When we ill-treat the land
     and forget we are God's stewards:
     O God, forgive us.

Declaration of Forgiveness

May God the Creator forgive our misusing of his creative work;
May God the Son take up into his cross the sufferings of our
land, our animals, our families and ourselves.
May God the Holy Spirit give us the strength and power to
overcome our troubles, weaknesses and temptations.
May God the Holy Trinity forgive us all our sins. **Amen.**

Hymn

'God, whose farm is all creation' (HO&N 236)

Our Gratitude for God's Gifts

All now stand and a representative of the Young Farmers, or other
person connected with the land, leads the people:

From God comes every good and perfect gift –
the rich soil, the smell of the fresh-turned earth:
Come from God.
The keenness of a winter's frost and our breath steaming:
Come from God.
The hum of the tractor, the gleam of a cutting edge:
Come from God.
The beauty of a clean-cut furrow,
the sweep of a well-ploughed field:
Come from God.
Blessed be God in all his gifts:
And praised by all his works.

Hymn

'Lord, bring the day to pass' (page 26)

An Address may be given.

Hymn

'For the beauty of the earth' (HO&N 184) *or*
'For the fruits of his creation' (HO&N 185)

A collection may be taken for a rural charity.

Blessing of the Plough

Towards the end of the hymn, representatives of farmers,
farm-workers and Young Farmers take their places around the
ploughshare.

All remain standing.

1st Speaker	The plough is the foundation of our work and a symbol of our labour:
2nd Speaker	For the soil to be broken up and the seed sown, we must first plough the fields.
3rd Speaker	For the green corn to grow and the ripe grain to be reaped, we must first plough the fields.
1st Speaker	For the bread to be baked and the people fed, we must first plough the fields.
2nd Speaker	For prosperity to come to our farms and families, we must first plough the fields.
3rd Speaker	So we bring this ploughshare here for you to give your blessing upon it and upon all the work done on our farms.
lst Speaker	God speed the plough: the plough and the ploughman, the farm and the farmer.
2nd Speaker	God speed the plough: the beam and the mouldboard, the slade and the sidecap, the share and the coulters.

3rd Speaker   God speed the plough:
in fair weather and foul,
in rain and wind,
in frost and sunshine:
God speed the plough.

Let us pray:

O God, who gives each of us work to do for your sake,
we ask for your blessing on this plough and upon all the
machines that enable us to do our work upon the land.
We ask you to prosper throughout the year
the work done on our local farms.
May the farmers' hopes be fulfilled in a plentiful harvest;
may your people be fed with wholesome food;
may town and country, united in gratitude to you,
be drawn nearer to the understanding
and true service of each other:
through Jesus Christ our Lord. **Amen.**

or

O God who has entrusted the soil to our keeping,
help us to give a good account of our management:
that as we keep our land in good heart,
so we may ourselves be kept rich in Christian living:
through Jesus Christ our Lord. **Amen.**

Blessing of the People and Dismissal

May God bless you in winter and summer,
at your ploughing, your sowing and your reaping.
May God give you sunshine and rain in due season;
May God, who gladdens the face of the earth,
give you joyfulness of heart.
May God, who has called you to work on the land,
set your affections upon himself.
And may the blessing of the Trinity,
three persons and one God,
remain with you and those you love for ever. **Amen.**

Silence is kept for a short time.

Hymn

'Immortal, invisible, God only wise' (HO&N 314)

The ploughshare may either be carried out at the end of the service in the same way as it was carried in, or be left in its place until everyone has gone.

Farm setting

Since modern ploughs are much too large to be moved about except with a tractor, an alternative is to go to a farm and set up a service there, perhaps out of doors in the autumn or in a farm building or machinery store. If the service is quite short there is no need to provide seating. Otherwise ask the family if they will put out some straw bales.

Preparation

Have personal invitations taken or sent to all farms in the neighbourhood and ask people from different farms to take the various turns as Speaker. Ask members of the local church or chapel to join in. Most people enjoy singing well-known hymns; if possible take a musician or group of musicians with you.

Choose some items from the service and start with the following lines:

Leader   We come in the name of the One who made us all, people, animals and the whole earth.

Farmer We welcome you and ask your blessing on the work we do here and all the work done on the farms around us.

It is good if, after the service, everyone can be invited to share some refreshments.

Hymns

O Christ who holds the open gate

O Christ who holds the open gate,
O Christ who drives the furrow straight,
O Christ, the plough, O Christ, the laughter
Of holy white birds flying after.

Lo, all my heart's field's red and torn,
And thou wilt bring the young green corn,
The young green corn divinely springing,
The young green corn for ever singing;

And when the field is fresh and fair
Thy blessed feet shall glitter there,
And we will walk the weeded field,
And tell the golden harvest's yield,

The corn that makes the holy bread
By which the soul of man is fed,
The holy bread, the food unpriced,
Thy everlasting mercy, Christ.

(John Masefield, 1878–1967)
Suggested tune: Wareham ('Jesus, where'er thy people meet')

Lord, bring the day to pass

Lord, bring the day to pass
When forest, rock and hill,
The beasts, the birds, the grass,
Will know your finished will.
When we attain your destiny
And nature lives in harmony.

Forgive our careless use
Of water, ore and soil –
The plenty we abuse
Supplied by others' toil.
Save us from making self our creed
Turn us towards each other's need.

Give us when we release
Creation's secret powers
To harness them for peace,
Our children's peace and ours:
Teach us the art of mastering
In servant form, which draws death's sting.

Creation groans, travails,
Futile its present plight,
Bound – till the hour it hails
God's children, born of light
Who enter on their true estate.
Come, Lord: new heavens and earth create.

(Ian M. Fraser, 1917– ; metre 66 66 66)
Suggested tune: Gopsal by Handel ('Rejoice, the Lord is king')

Blessing of Soil

This can take place during the Service for Plough Sunday. Otherwise it would be appropriate to have the blessing at an environmental or farming service. Arrange for a container of earth to be brought in, either from a local field or from a garden. Put ready a table or low platform, covered with a cloth. If there is a Sunday School, the cloth can be decorated by the children with pictures of plants and creatures that live in the soil. The container should be brought to the front, either at the beginning of the service or during the service with the following words:

> O Lord, we bring before you this soil,
> teeming with the life of tiny creatures,
> full of nutrients and goodness.
> Without soil no life would exist upon the earth.
> By it we are nourished and to it we will return.

Reading (based on Matthew 13.1–9)

This requires two voices.

A Where the soil is hard, neither ploughed nor forked,
the seed cannot take root and is eaten by the birds.

B Where the soil lies over rock with little depth,
the seeds fail to develop deep roots.
Plants spring up quickly but soon wither away.

A Where the soil is deeper but impoverished,
the seeds take root but the weeds grow more quickly
and choke the plants.

B Where the soil is well tended and fertile, in good heart,
the seed puts down deep roots, the plants grow tall
and strong and yield a rich harvest.

Prayer

A   O Lord, save us from hardness of heart,
where your word cannot take root.

B   O Lord, save us from shallowness of mind,
where your word withers away.

A   O Lord, save us from the deceitfulness of riches,
where your word is choked by everyday cares.

B   But Lord, grant that our hearts may be fertile soil,
where your word flourishes and yields a harvest,
bringing salvation to ourselves and those about us. **Amen.**

or

We give thanks for those who down the ages have studied
plants and soil, giving us a better understanding.
O let the earth bless the Lord:
Let it praise and magnify God for ever.
We give thanks for the satisfaction of growing good crops for
feeding beasts and people.
O let the earth bless the Lord:
Let it praise and magnify God for ever.
We give thanks for all growing things which provide us with
remedies and medicines.
O let the earth bless the Lord:
Let it praise and magnify God for ever.
We give thanks for all plants and trees which give us scent,
colour and beauty.
O let the earth bless the Lord:
Let it praise and magnify God for ever.

Blessing of the Soil

The Leader faces the congregation, scoops up a handful of soil in
a glass container and holds it up so that all can see it.

O Creator God, Maker of all that is,
we offer to you this soil;
we praise you
for this marvellous and intricate creation.

Help us to reverence and respect
the humble soil
as your chosen means of feeding
and providing for us.
Bless this soil and all the soil around us,
the soil in our fields and gardens,
the soil on the hills and in the woodlands,
so that the whole earth gives glory to you,
Creator, Son and Holy Spirit. **Amen.**

SPRING

Lambing Service

This service would be suitable for other occasions during the year where shepherds meet, such as at sheepdog trials.

The 'wisdom of the ewes' in the prayers refers to the good sense and innate knowledge that upland sheep at least are endowed with: they are said to be 'hefted' to their territory, knowing its boundaries, where to find water, which places are dangerous and which provide shelter and safety. This knowledge is imparted to their lambs, so they can pass it on in their turn. If sheep have to be brought in from outside, they have no local knowledge and there are more accidents and casualties. At first, the owner has to spend time every day rounding them up and bringing back any that have strayed – perhaps rather like the shepherd in the Parable of the Lost Sheep!

Welcome

Hymn

'The Lord's my shepherd' (HO&N 654)

Confession

Let us confess the faults and failings in our lives:

Eternal God, our Guide and Shepherd,
we have strayed from your ways like lost sheep.
We have not always loved our neighbours;
we have not always been good stewards
of the land and creatures in our care.
We trust in your son, Jesus Christ,
who on the cross took on himself
the sins and failings of us all.
Give us grace to amend our lives,
and faithfully follow in your ways. Amen.

Almighty God, who forgives all who truly repent,
have mercy upon you,
pardon and deliver you from all your sins,
confirm and strengthen you in all goodness,
and keep you in life eternal;
through Jesus Christ our Lord. **Amen.**

Hymn

'In heavenly love abiding' (HO&N 323) *or*

'Great God of all creation' (page 37)

Reading (Isaiah 40.9, 11; authors' own version)

Isaiah says the Lord is near and is a shepherd to his people.

You who bring good tidings to Zion,
go up on to a high mountain,
You who bring good tidings to Jerusalem,
lift up your voice with a shout,
lift it up, do not be afraid;
say to the cities of Judah:
Behold your God! Behold the Lord!
He looks after his flock like a shepherd,
he picks up the lambs in his arms,
and gently leads the pregnant ewes.

There are two alternatives for the next hymn and reading. The first is the hymn 'Father, hear the prayer we offer' with the 'Good Shepherd' reading; the second is the hymn 'There were ninety and nine' with the reading 'The Lost Sheep'.

Hymn

'Father, hear the prayer we offer' (HO&N 161)

Reading (John 10.14–16, NIV)

I am the good shepherd; I know my sheep and my sheep know me – just as the Father knows me and I know the Father – and I lay down my life for the sheep. I have other sheep that are not of this sheep pen. I must bring them also. They too will listen to my voice, and there shall be one flock and one shepherd.

or

Hymn

'There were ninety and nine' (page 36)

Reading (Luke 15.3–7, NIV)

Then Jesus told them this parable: 'Suppose one of you has a hundred sheep and loses one of them. Does he not leave the ninety-nine in the open country and go after the lost sheep until he finds it? And when he finds it, he joyfully puts it on his shoulders and goes home. Then he calls his friends and neighbours together and says, "Rejoice with me; I have found my lost sheep." I tell you that in the same way there is more rejoicing in heaven over one sinner who repents than over ninety-nine righteous persons who do not need to repent.'

Prayers

For the friendship and support of our communities,
for the beauty of hills and valleys:
We thank you, Lord of all.
For the changing weather and seasons,
the dawns and sunsets and the starry nights:
We thank you, Lord of all.
For the fields and pastures
which provide food for our flocks
and water from stream or river:
We thank you, Lord of all.
For our ewes, with their own wisdom;
for their strength and care as mothers:
We thank you, Lord of all.
For lambs, for the miracle of their birth,
and for the bounding joy of their young life:
We thank you, Lord of all.
We pray that our lambs may be free from sickness,
and safe from attack by animals and birds:
Lord, in your mercy:
Hear our prayer.

We pray that all who care for the sheep
may be given wisdom and endurance
and may receive a just reward for their work:
Lord, in your mercy:
Hear our prayer.

Hymn

'Thine for ever! God of love' (HO&N 673)

An Address may be given or a poem read (see end of service).

Hymn

'All creatures of our God and King' (HO&N 6) *or*
'O Lord, my God' (HO&N 511)

Final Prayer

O Creator God,
who has made us to live together,
to love one another
and to love the land on which we live:
we pray for ourselves,
that we may have the grace to preserve,
for those who come after,
the beauty of our landscape,
the traditions of our people,
and the strength of our local community. **Amen.**

Blessing

The God of peace,
who brought again from the dead our Lord Jesus Christ,
that great shepherd of the sheep,
make you perfect in every good work to do his will.
And the blessing of God almighty,
be among you and remain with you always. **Amen.**

Hymns

There were ninety and nine that safely lay

There were ninety and nine that safely lay
In the shelter of the fold;
But one was out on the hills away
Far from the gates of gold,
Away on the mountains wild and bare,
Away from the tender Shepherd's care.

Lord, thou hast here thy ninety and nine;
Are they not enough for thee?
But the Shepherd made answer: 'This of mine
Has wandered away from me;
And although the road be rough and steep,
I go to the desert to find my sheep.'

But none of the ransomed ever knew
How deep were the waters crossed,
Nor how dark was the night that the Lord passed through,
Ere he found his sheep that was lost.
Out in the desert he heard its cry,
Sick and helpless and ready to die.

Lord, whence are those blood-drops all the way
That mark out the mountain's track?
They were shed for one who had gone astray,
Ere the Shepherd could bring him back.
Lord, whence are thy hands so rent and torn?
They are pierced tonight by many a thorn.

And all through the mountains, thunder-riven,
And up from the rocky steep,
There rose a cry to the gate of heaven:
Rejoice, I have found my sheep.
And the angels echoed around the throne:
Rejoice, for the Lord brings back his own.

(Elizabeth C. Clephane, 1830–69; metre 97 97 99)
Tune: Ninety and Nine (*English Hymnal* 584)

Great God of all creation

Great God of all creation,
Dear Lord of plain and hill,
Of wisdom and of knowledge,
All learning and all skill,
We worship and adore thee
With humble hearts again
That by thy loving kindness,
Man's work is not in vain.

As every new invention,
Is teaching us more skill,
Give us the grace to use them,
According to thy will,
That none may need to hunger
And earth become more fair,
With bounteous gifts of harvest
For all the world to share.

For herdsman and for shepherd,
We ask a special prayer,
That every gentle creature
Committed to their care
May live in quiet comfort
Supplying all our need,
And never be exploited
To satisfy man's greed.

We thank thee, gracious Father,
For all thy love provides,
With ever-growing wonder
For all that earth supplies,
Rich tokens of thy kindness
Throughout the world we see.
With grateful hearts we offer
Our love and praise to thee.

(Mrs L. M. Porch; metre 76 76 D)

Suggested tunes: Wir pflügen ('We plough the fields'); Morning light
('Stand up, stand up for Jesus'); Cruger ('Hail to the Lord's anointed');
St Theodulph ('All glory, laud and honour')

Poems

The Lamb

Little Lamb, who made thee?
Dost thou know who made thee?
Gave thee life, and bid thee feed
By the stream and o'er the mead;
Gave thee clothing of delight,
Softest clothing, woolly, bright;
Gave thee such a tender voice,
Making all the vales rejoice?
Little Lamb, who made thee?
Dost thou know who made thee?

Little Lamb, I'll tell thee,
Little Lamb, I'll tell thee;
He is callèd by thy name,
For He calls Himself a Lamb.
He is meek, and He is mild;
He became a little child.
I a child, and thou a lamb,
We are callèd by His name.
Little Lamb, God bless thee!
Little Lamb, God bless thee!

(William Blake, 1757–1827)

We Like Sheep

Sheep will stray together
Through bank or stream or hollow,
Just one will find the weakest place,
And all the rest will follow.

Sheep will take no tempting,
No clinging to their master;
Another voice will sound as sweet
And to a sweeter pasture.

Sheep are never free from danger,
Always prone to plunder,
Stolen, lost or set upon,
No matter what their number.

Lord, make me understand
and keep myself from falling;
Not to follow other sheep
But hear my Shepherd calling.

(Wilf Ward, 1948–)

In Praise of Collie

She was a small dog, neat and fluid –
Even her conversation was tiny:
She greeted you with *bow*, never *bow-wow*.

Her sons stood monumentally over her
But did what she told them. Each grew grizzled
'Til it seemed he was his own mother's grandfather.

Once, gathering sheep on a showery day,
I remarked how dry she was. Pollochan said 'Ah,
It would take a very accurate drop to hit Lassie.'

And her tact – and tactics! When the sheep bolted
In an unforeseen direction, over the skyline
Came – who but Lassie and not even panting.

She sailed in the dinghy like a proper sea-dog.
Where's a burn? – She's first on the other side.
She flowed through fences like a piece of black wind.

But suddenly she was old and sick and crippled . . .
I grieved for Pollochan when he took her for a stroll
And put his gun to the back of her head.

(Norman MacCaig, 1910–96)

Clypping Service

History

An interesting link with the Roman occupation of this country is the ceremony of 'yclepping' (the ancient name) or 'clypping', that is, embracing or hugging the church, when the congregation and parishioners form a ring around their parish church and embrace it.

The ceremony is probably of Roman origin. At a time when Britain was mainly a land of unenclosed uplands, flatland and forested valleys, the sheep and goats on which the inhabitants relied were the prey of predators such as wolves. To protect themselves and their animals, people sought the aid of their gods. They used the ancient feast of Lupercalia, which was dedicated to the wolf-god Lycian Pan, celebrated in Rome itself and as far north as Gaul. The feast was held in February, near the onset of the mating season. Goats and young dogs were sacrificed and the young people of the village danced round the altar.

The coming of Christianity ended the sacrifices and the rites associated with them but the Church christianized this ceremony instead of abolishing it entirely. In the fifth century, the festival of Lupercalia became associated with the Purification of the Virgin Mary on 2 February. Later on it became associated with Mothering Sunday and patronal festivals.

There were always many local customs and traditions, but the dancing of children during the encircling was very common. Often too the clypping was allied with local fairs, some of which were held in the churchyard. However, the holding of secular fairs in churchyards was ended by an Act of Parliament in the reign of Edward I.

Clypping died out at one time but there has been a revival of interest in the nineteenth and twentieth centuries. At present services are taking place in at least eleven English counties, and there is interest in other counties and also in New Zealand.

Favourite hymns are: 'The Church's one foundation', 'Praise my soul the King of Heaven', and 'We love the place, O God'.

Preparation

If there are not enough people, then provide:

1.   a rope that will surround the building. The people can hold it at intervals and stand still while singing; or

2.   a shorter rope, which is held at intervals as above but people walk round the building while they sing; or

3.   lengths of ribbon or tape which link everyone together. People either stand still or walk round the building while they sing.

Arrange for three speakers to say the prayers on pages 44–5 and for three people to light the candles. Before the service, put the candles on some kind of stand or table with heatproof covering.

This service is suitable for town as well as country and should appeal to children as well as adults. An alternative way of doing the clypping is to stay inside and 'embrace' the main part of the church.

....

Hymn

'Praise my soul the King of Heaven' (HO&N 565) *or*
'Onward Christian families' (page 46)

Welcome

The Lord be with you:
And also with you.

Verses from Hebrews 12.1, 2

Since we are surrounded by so great a cloud of witnesses, let us throw off everything that hinders us . . .
Let us fix our eyes on Jesus, the author and perfecter of our faith. (Hebrews 12.1, 2, NIV)

or

Verses adapted from Galatians 4.24ff

Isaac was the son of Abraham
by Sarah, who was a free woman.
Our mother is the heavenly Jerusalem
and she is free with all her children.
Like Isaac, we are children of promise
and share in the same inheritance.

A few words about the service

We have come here today to praise God for all his blessings
in our daily lives and in our Christian community,
to rededicate ourselves to his service
and to pray for his continued grace and guidance.
Firstly let us acknowledge our failings
and our need for forgiveness.

Responses

We have been shy about declaring the wonder of your love:
Lord, have mercy.
We have been lukewarm in our love for our families and our
community:
Lord, have mercy.
We have been hesitant in offering our service to those in need:
Lord, have mercy.

Let us now praise God.
For our baptism and new birth in Christ:
We thank you, O Lord.
For Holy Communion and all the worship in this place:
We thank you, O Lord.
For the blessings of Christian marriage and home life:
We thank you, O Lord.
For the faithful departed and the communion of saints:
We thank you, O Lord.
For the joys of creation and the beauty of our world:
We thank you, O Lord.
Glory, honour and praise be yours:
Now and for ever. Amen.

or

> O God, giver of all good things,
> we praise you for the blessings given through
> the worldwide family of Christian believers;
> we bless you for the grace given through Communion
> and for our fellowship in Christ with one another;
> we thank you for the teaching of the scriptures
> and the preaching of your word;
> also for the example of those known to us
> who have departed this life in your faith;
> through Jesus Christ our Lord. **Amen.**

Hymn

'The Church's one foundation' (HO&N 636) *or*
'For I'm building a people of power' (HO&N 181)

Reading (verses from John 15, NRSV)

> I am the true vine, and my Father is the vine-grower. He
> removes every branch in me that bears no fruit. Every branch
> that bears fruit he prunes to make it bear more fruit . . . Just as
> the branch cannot bear fruit by itself unless it abides in the
> vine, neither can you unless you abide in me. I am the vine,
> you are the branches. Those who abide in me and I in them
> bear much fruit . . . If you abide in me, and my words abide in
> you, ask for whatever you wish, and it will be done for you. My
> Father is glorified by this, that you bear much fruit and
> become my disciples. As the Father has loved me, so I have
> loved you; abide in my love . . . I have said these things to you
> so that my joy may be in you, and that your joy may be
> complete.

An Address may be given or the following poem read:

Poem: i am a little church

i am a little church(no great cathedral)
far from the splendour and squalor of hurrying cities
—i do not worry if briefer days grow briefest,
i am not sorry when sun and rain make april

my life is the life of the reaper and the sower;
my prayers are prayers of earth's own clumsily striving
(finding and losing and laughing and crying)children
whose any sadness or joy is my grief or my gladness

around me surges a miracle of unceasing
birth and glory and death and resurrection:
over my sleeping self float flaming symbols
of hope,and i wake to a perfect patience of mountains

i am a little church(far from the frantic
world with its rapture and anguish)at peace with nature
—i do not worry if longer nights grow longest;
i am not sorry when silence becomes singing

winter by spring,i lift my diminutive spire to
merciful Him Whose only now is forever:
standing erect in the deathless truth of His presence
(welcoming humbly His light and proudly His darkness)

(E. E. Cummings, 1894–1962)

Prayers

1st Speaker Let us pray for our Christian community.

Lord of all power and might,
renew all your followers in this place
in their vocation and faithfulness.
Fill us with your Holy Spirit
so that we declare the wonder
of your love to all the world;
through Jesus Christ our Saviour. **Amen.**

2nd Speaker Let us pray for the spirit of service.

> Lord Jesus Christ,
> who took the form of a servant
> and became human for our sake:
> give us the same spirit of service
> and help us to follow in your steps,
> that with love and humility
> we may give ourselves to those who need our help
> and thus fulfil the commands of the gospel,
> to the glory of your name. **Amen.**

3rd Speaker Let us pray for home and family life.

> O God, whose Son shared the life of an earthly home,
> send down your blessing upon our homes.
> Grant to parents wisdom and perseverance
> and to children the spirit of respect and obedience.
> Unite our families in the bond of mutual love
> and in showing patience, generosity
> and all the fruits of the Spirit
> in our life together;
> through Jesus Christ, our Lord. **Amen.**

or

Responses

1st Speaker Let us pray for the Christian community in this place.

The first candle is lit and there is a short silence.

> Lord, in your mercy:
> **Hear our prayer.**

2nd Speaker Let us pray for the spirit of service.

The second candle is lit and there is a short silence.

> Lord, in your mercy:
> **Hear our prayer.**

3rd Speaker Let us pray for home and family life.

The third candle is lit and there is a short silence.

> Lord, in your mercy:
> **Hear our prayer.**

Let us sum up all our prayers by saying together our family prayer:

The Lord's Prayer (page 227)

Hymn

'One more step along the world I go' (HO&N 525) *or*
'We love the place O God' (HO&N 718) *or*
'Bind us together' (HO&N 72)

During the singing of this hymn, the leader (and choir) leads everyone outside or into a circle inside the building. Once everyone is in place, either holding hands, or lifting the rope or being linked with ribbon or tape, one of the other hymns is sung.

Hymn

'We love the place O God' (HO&N 718) *or*
'One more step along the world I go' (HO&N 525) *or*
'Bind us together, Lord' (HO&N 72)

Everyone gathers outside the main door and says together:

The grace of our Lord Jesus Christ,
and the love of God,
and the fellowship of the Holy Spirit,
be with us now and evermore. Amen.

Go in peace to love and serve the Lord:
In the name of Christ. Amen.

Hymn

Onward Christian families

Onward Christian families,
Sing a happy song,
Lifting hearts and voices
As you march along.
Festal banners waving,

Young and old adore
Father, Son and Holy Spirit,
God for evermore.
Chorus after each verse: first four lines of verse 1.

For that home at Nazareth
Hear our songs of praise:
For all those who shared in
Jesus' boyhood days.
Praise too for his manhood
When in Joseph's trade
In his home and local district
His full part he played.
Chorus

Onward, Christian pilgrims,
As through life you roam,
Sing a song of gladness
For a Christian home,
For the love that binds you,
For the things you share,
For the laughter, tears and friendships
And the constant care.
Chorus

Onward, Christian families,
Sing a joyful song
For that greater family
To which we all belong.
Sprinkled with the water
In the threefold name
Of the holy Church of Jesus
Membership we claim.
Chorus

(Author unknown)
Tune: St Gertrude

Palm Sunday

Background

The triumphal entry fulfils the prophecy from the Old Testament,
'Behold your king comes to you . . . humble and sitting upon an
ass, upon a colt, the foal of an ass' (Zechariah 9.9–10). At that
time in the Middle East the horse was normally only used in war
and so the use of a donkey was a sign that Jesus came in peace.

Looking down on a donkey's back, you can see a dark stripe in
the shape of a cross, running from ears to tail and from shoulder
to shoulder. As Jesus looked down, he would see the cross as a
reminder of what was to come, and Christians too are reminded
in this way of the holy function of this humble animal.

The hymn most often used for a procession is 'All glory, laud and
honour' (HO&N 14). Other suggestions are: 'Ride on, ride on in
majesty (HO&N 583); 'Hosanna' from *Jesus Christ Superstar*; 'My
song is love unknown' (HO&N 463); 'We have a king who rides a
donkey' (HO&N 905).

A simple Palm Sunday procession

The simplest form of procession is with a led donkey
accompanied by a crowd of worshippers singing and possibly
waving 'palms'. If you have a rider, it is more effective if both the
rider and the person leading the donkey wear costume,
preferably a bright tunic and cloak. As 'Jesus' will be riding
astride, he should wear something fairly loose.

At the start, use the following words (Zechariah 9.9–10, NIV):

> Rejoice greatly, O Daughter of Zion,
> Shout, Daughter of Jerusalem!
> See, your king comes to you,

righteous and having salvation,
gentle and riding on a donkey,
on a colt, the foal of a donkey.

Or else the following prayer:

We have come here today
to witness to our Christian faith,
and to walk in the steps of our Lord
to the foot of the cross.
We pray that as we do so,
we may find ourselves closer to him
and more deeply thankful
for his saving death and resurrection. **Amen.**

The words of Zechariah or the prayer can be repeated at places
en route where new people are joining in.

At end of a procession with a donkey:

O Lord Jesus Christ,
whose sign of the cross we see
on the back of [*name of donkey*],
we thank you for giving us living creatures
as companions in our work and leisure;
give us the grace to see
that in their response and humble service,
they point us to you, their Lord and Master,
who died for us and all creation upon the cross
and now lives in glory. **Amen.**

Good Friday

Introduction

Christians tend to think of the crucifixion and resurrection primarily as redeeming humanity, saving it from the power of sin and death, but from Paul's letters we can see that these events touched the whole of God's creation:

> For God was pleased to have all his fulness dwell in him, and through him to reconcile to himself all things, whether things on earth or things in heaven, by making peace through his blood, shed on the cross. (Colossians 1.20, NIV)

> The creation was subjected to frustration, not by its own choice, but by the will of the one who subjected it, in hope that the creation itself will be liberated from its bondage to decay and brought into the glorious freedom of the children of God. (Romans 8.20–1, NIV)

There is plenty of devotional material available dwelling on the events of Good Friday and the effect they have on our lives. We have therefore concentrated on events as affecting the non-human creation.

Alternatives to services in church or chapel

Outdoor processions have now become popular. The procession can start from some local spot and end up at the church or chapel, be on a circular route or start from a place of worship, taking a cross up to a local landmark. A procession or pilgrimage involving a number of different venues is given on page 53–5.

Observance of Good Friday

In days gone by, Good Friday was a day when all businesses, shops and other facilities were closed and there was very little traffic. Then came a time when it became an ordinary working day for most people. Now at least it is a Bank Holiday and many places of work are closed.

How can we, as Christians, make something more of Good Friday than a mere holiday? Certainly by attending a service and perhaps by not going shopping but doing quiet things at home or finding time for reflection. Traditional food is always helpful in creating a sense of occasion and hot cross buns are the obvious choice. If your service is in the afternoon, the buns can be served with a cup of tea afterwards or else make tea a family occasion at home.

Suitable activities for children are:

- making hot cross buns;
- planting seeds – an old tradition, connected to the words of Jesus: 'Unless a grain of wheat falls into the ground and dies' (John 12.24), and also of course his burial;
- preparing an Easter garden at home;
- making Easter cards.

The following Responses and Prayer are suitable for an outdoor or rural setting.

Responses

Before Christ's sacrifice on the cross:
Bulls and goats were sacrificed for sin.
The old covenant needed blood from animals:
The shedding of blood brought forgiveness.
Now Christ has brought forgiveness of our sins:
By the shedding of his own blood on the cross.
Now animals as well as we ourselves:
Have received a new covenant.
No longer is their blood required:
Forgiveness comes through the blood of Christ.
His sacrifice was made once for all:
And we have been made holy by it.

Prayer

O lamb of God,
who takes away the sin of the world,
we praise and exalt you,
for in our new relationship with you,
we have a new relationship with your creatures. Amen.

or

Responses

When Jesus hung upon the cross:
The natural creation grieved.
Creation mourned its Lord:
It mourned the Lord of all the earth.
We too are dust of earth:
And children of the same Creator.
Brother sun and sister earth:
Share with us frustration.
They are constrained by failure and decay:
They long to be freed and made new,
To glorify our God:
In beauty, peace and joy.

O Lord of life,
hanging upon a tree,
pierced by metal nails,
we give you thanks;
by your death you have destroyed death
and have given us abundant life. Amen.

Procession of witness

Background

This procession or pilgrimage was devised for a combined group of five parishes which consists of six villages, one hamlet and one additional churchyard (the church burnt down in 1666 and was never rebuilt).

It is a way of involving all ages and drawing in members of the visited communities who might not otherwise attend church on Good Friday.

The core group travels round in cars and is joined at each location by local residents. The same sequences could be used at different locations within walking distance, with the cross carried from place to place. In this way it would be suitable for an urban setting.

Preparation

Publicize the event within your chosen area by means of posters and leaflets giving time and place for each section.

Construct a cross that will fit into a large estate car or trailer once it is assembled. Hammer in nails where the hands and feet would be. Find 'cross-bearers/supporters' for each location.

Also needed are:

- a towel;
- a bread roll or loaf and a bunch of grapes, both with red ribbon threaded through, so they can be hung on the arms of the cross;
- 30 'pieces of silver' and a small leather or similar pouch with a loop for hanging it up on the cross;
- a scourge with a loop on its handle, made by a member of the congregation;
- a crown of thorns;
- some large nails and a piece of wood (out of sight of those present, someone should hammer these into the wood at the appropriate moment – it is the *sound* which is the important symbol and it is a very powerful moment indeed).

Each session follows the same pattern:

- reading;
- action – construct the cross at the first location and thereafter add the appropriate symbol;
- prayer and/or brief meditation;
- hymn.

The times below give some idea of how long it takes to visit seven locations, covering a distance of some 28 miles.

For the hymns, if outdoors, either sing unaccompanied or persuade local musicians to come with you (on one occasion, a brass duo accompanied the core group). If indoors, a piano or organ can provide accompaniment.

Time	12 noon
Place	On a village green
Reading	Acts 10.38–43
Action	Construct the cross
Time	12.30 p.m.
Place	Outside a church (or inside if wet)
Reading	John 13.3–17
Action	Hang towel round cross
Time	1 p.m.
Place	In a churchyard
Reading	Matthew 26.26–30
Action	Affix bread and grapes
Time	1.20 p.m.
Place	In courtyard of a former farm
Reading	Matthew 26.14–16
Action	Count out the money, place in pouch and hang on cross
Time	1.45 p.m.
Place	In the open air outside a church
Reading	Matthew 27.21–6
Action	Affix scourge
Time	2.15 p.m.
Place	Inside a church
Reading	Mark 15.16–20
Action	Place crown of thorns over top of cross

Time   2.40 p.m.
Place   Inside a church
Reading   Mark 15.20b–39
Action   Hammer in nails (see earlier notes)

In the final hymn, the cross is lifted high by a 'cross-bearer'.

The act of worship ends with a blessing and is followed by tea and hot cross buns in the village hall or elsewhere, arranged by local people.

Some years the weather is kinder than others, so it's useful to have indoor venues available or, better still, keep going with your umbrellas – it is an act of witness as well as worship!

Cross, nails and crown of thorns

The following is suitable for integrating into a Good Friday service of readings and meditations.

1

A large wooden cross is placed at the front of the worship area together with a hammer and a box of nails.

During the service a meditation is read which deals with a particular situation in the world: famine; war; environmental destruction; homelessness; drugs and alcohol abuse; child poverty; religious intolerance; race relations; abortion; minority rights . . . the list is endless, but it is important to select no more than about eight or nine at the most.

After each meditation/reading a member of the congregation goes to the front and hammers a nail into the cross to symbolize our ongoing crucifixion of Christ in the modern world and day-to-day lives.

Suitable music could be played very quietly in the background, for example Gorecki's 'Three Sad Songs', but this is equally powerful when done in total silence.

On Easter morning flowers and ribbons are fastened to the nails to symbolize the resurrection of Christ.

2

Here a table is set in the place of the cross and on this is set a crown of thorns; hawthorn or blackthorn are both suitable. A hammer and large nails are again provided.

The process is similar to that above but instead of driving nails into a cross they are symbolically placed in the crown of thorns. On Saturday the nails are removed and fastened together in pairs to form a small cross which is then given to each person as they enter for a sunset-to-sunrise vigil.

On Easter morning each person is given a flower or a candle to take away with them as well as the cross of nails. Again this symbolizes the death and resurrection of Christ.

A little play for Holy Week

The whole creation was altered by thy passion;
for all things suffered with thee, knowing, O Lord,
that thou holdest all things in unity.

(Byzantine Rite)

Background

The above quotation might explain why a drama with characters such as a donkey, a dog, a tree and a stone appears in this book. We might also reflect on the story of Noah and the ensuing covenant with all creation, or on Balaam and his donkey, together with other Old Testament passages where the fates of the natural and human creation are linked.

The play looks at a familiar story from a new perspective. It appeals to the younger generation but also makes an impact on people who don't go to services. It is suitable for town and country.

Performing the play

It can be done in a church or chapel, a school or village hall. Costumes can be as simple or as elaborate as time and talent permit. At the very least, the animals need ears or masks and perhaps gloves, the tree needs some branches, either real or made out of cardboard, and the stone can be covered in a grey blanket.

With younger children, the text can be shortened, but if too much is taken out, it will lose some of its impact. For older children, the words can either be learnt by heart or put on cards.

Start with a well-known hymn if possible: 'There is a green hill far away' (HO&N 657) is a good choice, followed by a short talk about the first Good Friday, then about what is going to be seen today. This can refer to Balaam, as above, and how the work of Jesus affects the whole of God's creation, of which we are a part and on which we depend for our very lives.

Finish with a blessing and another well-known hymn, followed if possible by drinks and hot cross buns.

Characters

- the donkey that carried Jesus into Jerusalem on Palm Sunday;
- a stray dog;
- a tree near the tomb;
- the stone which covered the entrance to the tomb.

Donkey   How do you think, then, that I felt, I who carried him in triumph? At first, when those two men came to fetch me, I didn't want to go. I stood on my hind legs and tried to run away, but they were too strong for me. One pulled on my rope and the other pushed me from behind. But when I reached *him*, then I knew! One touch of his hand on my head and I recognized my Creator and my Lord, one I would go with, though it cost my life. We went through pushing, shouting crowds, but I wasn't frightened. The crowds were waving branches which almost touched my head, but I never flinched. The garments on the road felt strange beneath my feet, but I never hesitated.

Tree   My cousins stand along the road from Bethany. *They* knew he was their Creator and their Lord, Brother Donkey. With people taking branches to wave, they too felt that they were praising him and sharing in his triumph.

Dog   You weren't the only creature who felt his touch. Me, a stray dog, who no one has time for, who has to scavenge food or go without, often getting more kicks than food. I saw him on that day of triumph, but it was another day when he spoke to me and touched me and I felt his love for all the poor and outcasts. His friends didn't like me; they tried to push me away but he made sure I shared in what they had.

Donkey   All that week I lived as in a dream. I saw my Lord when he came out to Bethany at night after a day in the city. He laid his hand upon my head and gave me peace, but I could feel heaviness in his touch, and a sense of foreboding.

Dog   Yes, there was a very strange atmosphere in the city. He walked around and talked with many people, even laughed, but when I came close to him, I felt the heaviness.

Stone   I suppose you don't think that stones have any voice – oh, no, they're just boring old stones, lying around and of little use, unless you want to build a house or wall. You don't know the half of it. I heard them talking, them as thinks themselves better than other people, when they walked by last week. 'What a performance,' one said; 'All those people, where did they come from? Badly behaved as well, pushing and shoving, tearing down branches and making such a noise.' 'Yes, I managed to get close to this Jesus,' said the other, 'and told him to shut them up, and do you know what he said? "If they were quiet, the very stones would cry out."' So there you are, it's official, from the horse's mouth as you might say.

Donkey   Four nights he came to Bethany. I looked for him on the fifth night; there were lights and noise in the darkness, but he never came.

Dog   That night I waited outside the house where they all gathered and I feasted on what they'd left. I followed when they left the house. I saw his friends all fall asleep while he went away and prayed and groaned in anguish. I wanted to go and lick his hand but I didn't dare approach at such an hour. I saw the soldiers come and take him; his friends all ran away. I followed but not too closely – I thought I'd only get kicked.

Donkey And then that dreadful day. I heard the sounds of shouting but not like the other day. It seemed to me like the roaring of wild beasts, but worse, because I knew it was people and not beasts. I stood disturbed in a corner of my field. The roaring seemed to fill my ears, though it must have been several miles away.

Dog Yes, I heard the turmoil too. I crept near to Pilate's house but had no heart to hear and watch what happened there. Later I heard the tramp of Roman feet and the mocking cries that followed them.

Donkey At noon, the sun hid his face and darkness fell; blacker and blacker went the world, all birds stopped singing, dogs started howling and people, even strong men, started wailing. I crowded close to my friends but there was no comfort in it. We were lost in thick darkness, a shapeless void; it felt deathly cold – was this the end of the world?

Dog When the world went black, the darkness pressed upon me so I could hardly breathe. I howled and then found the littlest corner that there was and curled myself inside it with my tail over my eyes and mouth, and waited, as I thought, for death.

Tree My little friends, I stood close by and was a witness of that day. In the darkness, I stretched my branches heavenward to seek for comfort, but there was none. The air was full of whirring wings; I saw nothing but I felt dark powers beating upon that cross, to tear the man off before his work was done. I heard thunder and waited for a lightning bolt to strike and cleave my trunk.

Donkey How long the darkness lasted I don't know, but as the light returned, I heard a voice, so loud it nearly

deafened me and it cried that all was done, the work
accomplished; then the earth shook as though it were
adrift in space. I felt it right through my body to the
tips of my ears, flattened against my neck in fear and
misery. After that – nothing, but I still felt cold and lost,
as though no one loved me, as though love itself was
gone from the world.

Tree   I also heard the cry, which seemed to go through every
fibre of my being. When the ground shook, I trembled
to my roots, waited for the soil and rocks to give way so
that I would crash to earth. But stillness came and
sounds of weeping. The light returned and the dark
powers fled by, baulked of their purpose.

Dog   I thought the earthquake was the death-throes of our
world. After it was over and the light returned, I didn't
want to stay in the city, where people went about
dismayed, not looking at each other.

Tree   After a while my limbs stopped trembling and I saw a
sad procession coming, with men and women, and a
body on a bier, covered with a bloody cloth. As they
passed, I bent my branches to the earth in mourning; I
knew the world had changed and nothing would be the
same any more, not for me, not for the creatures living
in and around me, and especially not for the humans
who walked beneath.

Stone   I heard the thunder, and the shaking of the earth went
through me, so violent that I was rolled from my place
beside the tomb. The procession you saw came and
stopped beside me. They were in haste because the
hour was late, not long before the beginning of the
Sabbath, when nothing moves. Two men, richly
dressed, directed servants to wind the body in clean
strips of cloth. I saw his face, pallid and bloody, but
peaceful and somehow triumphant. His head was
wrapped in a separate cloth and then the body placed
inside the tomb. The women stood apart and watched.
All the men pushed me and I rolled into place as a seal,
then everyone went away.

Dog   I felt I couldn't stay in the city and I went out into the countryside. The Sabbath started and I saw no one. I felt alone, bereft. I was hungry but there was no one to feed me. I was thirsty but there was no one to give me a drink.

Stone   Yesterday, when the Sabbath rest was over, some other men appeared, the temple guard who'd been told to keep a watch. It seemed like the end, but the end of what? I felt cold and lifeless, dense and heavy. Would I just stand there ages long, while the bones inside the tomb mouldered into dust and the world went on its way, unforgiving and unforgiven?

All was peaceful until the early hours of this morning. Suddenly I was aware of a presence in the tomb, alive, electric, and then I felt all my particles expand and vibrate as if I were stretched beyond my natural state. Something passed through me, leaving me tingling in every part. At that the earth shook violently and I was thrown back beyond the entrance to the tomb. The guards fled and when women came to tend the body, I knew they'd find nothing, for *he* was alive.

Donkey   Today everything is different. Very early, when all the cocks were crowing, I too felt the earth shake once more, but it was as though it leapt for joy. The grass tasted sweeter, the water from the stream purer. We all leapt and gambolled and brayed, even my staid mother and her friends with their stiff limbs. As the day wore on, I knew that my Master was with me once more, that he'd always be with me and he wanted me to serve him by serving those around me.

Dog   Yes – today, I too know that I have a Master and he is alive; the whole city is somehow aware of his presence which lies over it like a golden glow. Even his friends, the ones who had no time for me, are transformed – when I went back to that house, they welcomed me and gave me food and drink. I feel loved in a way I'd never known before, not even as a small puppy with my family.

Tree   Today, my bark is warm and silken, my fibres seem to sing and my branches stretch themselves out as though they would grow longer, stronger, while the leaves pulse with sap and vitality. I will stand here, gladly giving what I have – shade from the heat of the day, a place to rest and beauty to delight the eye.

Stone   This day has been like nothing I've ever experienced in all my millennia, and, as you say, Sister Tree, the world has changed, nothing will ever be the same again. Even the sun seems to shine with a greater glow and glory, giving praise to him who is the Lord of life.

All   **Praise to him who is the Lord of life.**

Easter Day

Acclamations

Alleluia!
Christ is the image of the invisible God,
the firstborn over all creation;
and through him God was pleased
to reconcile to himself all things,
whether on earth or in heaven,
by making peace through the blood of his cross.
Alleluia!

Responsive Acclamations

These can be used separately or during a Communion Service,
either in the Intercessory Section or after the Communion.

Now is Christ risen from the dead:
the first fruits of them that slept, Alleluia!

In a garden God first put us
to live in peace and joy.
In a garden God suffered tears
and sweat of agony.
In a garden
God rose to life
and restored to all creation
life and joy and peace.
O gardens with new life,
rejoice with us. Alleluia!

When Christ rode into Jerusalem,
the stones were ready to cry out
and proclaim him Lord of all creation.

When Christ died on the cross,
the earth shook and the rocks split
to share the loss and devastation.
When Christ was buried in a tomb of rock
the stone was rolled away,
rejoicing to reveal
the glory of our risen Lord.
O earth and stones and rocks,
rejoice with us. Alleluia!

When Jesus preached in Galilee,
his seamless robe revealed
our love and care for him.
When Jesus died upon the cross,
the temple curtain tore
to show the direct way to God.
When Jesus rose again,
the linen cloths gave witness
to God's power and saving love.
O all things we have created
in love for Christ our Lord,
rejoice with us. Alleluia!

O let all things visible and invisible,
earthly and heavenly,
all people, tribes and nations,
saved by the blood of Christ
join with us to praise and glorify
the Lord of all creation.
He left his heavenly throne
to suffer with us and release his damaged creation
from death, sin and decay,
that we might be in Paradise with him
and live for ever in his joy and peace.
Alleluia! Glory to our Saviour!
Alleluia! Glory to our Maker!
Alleluia! Glory to our God!

Prayers

Opening Prayer

O God, who by your mighty power
raised your Son Jesus Christ from the dead,
and released us and the whole creation
from death, futility and sin,
we join with all creation
to give you praise and glory
for the hope of our own resurrection
and the new heaven and new earth
which you will create. **Alleluia!**

Suggested 'Preface' before 'Holy, Holy, Holy' in Eucharistic Prayer

. . . And now we give you thanks because
the whole creation rejoices in new life
and the glorious hope of its re-creation in heaven;
and we ourselves have been saved from sin and death
by his bitter passion and mighty resurrection . . .

Final Prayer

O God, who saw that the only way
to break the power of sin and death
over us and over all creation
was to come in person and suffer with us;
breathe on us your Holy Spirit,
that going out from here in joy
and love for all your creation,
we may spread the good news
to all the world. **Amen.**

or

O God, we praise you
for redeeming your whole creation
from sin, death and decay,

by coming to earth to take
your sufferings on yourself,
and by your almighty power
raising your Son from the dead.
We go out from here in joy
ready to do everything we do
in the name of the Lord Jesus. **Alleluia. Amen.**

Blessing

Go out into the world
in the joy and peace
of the resurrection of the Lord Jesus.
Care for his redeemed creation;
follow him as children of the light;
make disciples by your life and words;
and glorify him by your dedication and love;
so may he bless you with his gift of the Holy Spirit
and be with you until his kingdom comes. **Alleluia. Amen.**

Hymn

Like sunrise on the purple skies

Like sunrise on the purple skies
Did Jesus from the grave arise
With life and light and splendour,
So though we still return to dust,
Within his kingdom winter must
To heav'nly spring surrender.

As songbirds in the sunny spring
O'er fields and forest sweetly sing
Of life and light returning,
Let every tongue sing out his praise
Who conquered death and brought us grace
From God on Easter morning!

As lilies open white and gold,
As grain is growing, leaves unfold
By gentle springtime powers.
So life in Jesus' name shall grow
In hearts and home-life here below
And save this world of ours.

(N. F. S. Grundtvig, 1846; *Songs from Denmark*; metre 88 78 87)
Suggested tune: Evening Hymn by William Jackson

An alternative is 'Easter Carol' from *Oxford Book of Carols*.

Reading

This reading is also suitable for Harvest. You may have two voices reading alternate lines, or use the reading as a responsorial one.

A	The earth is ploughed, the ground prepared
B	The prophets spake his word.
A	The seed is sown
B	A star shines bright across the earth.
A	The shoots of new life appear
B	Jesus, our Lord is here.
A	The stem grows strong and tall
B	The Son proclaims the Father's love.
A	The grain swells and ripens
B	Miracles of love performed.
A	The wheat is cut down
B	Jesus, Christ, is crucified.
A	The grain is stored
B	Jesus, our Lord, is dead and buried.
A	The flour is ground, the bread is made
B	His body and blood to us is offered.
A	'Eat, drink in remembrance of me' –
B	Jesus Christ lives!

(Author unknown)

Eastern Orthodox Easter Customs

From Ash Wednesday throughout the period of Lent, Orthodox Christians eat only bread, fruit and vegetables, and drink water.

Then during the time leading up to Easter, families will bake special cakes using eggs, and make savoury dishes using meat and other foods that they have not eaten during Lent.

All these things, together with brightly painted eggs, will be taken to church on Holy Saturday night. At midnight, as the day of Jesus's resurrection is welcomed, prayers will be said over all the carefully prepared food and it will be taken back to the people's homes, to be eaten as part of the joy of Easter Day.

The eggs will be distributed after the service. People crack eggs together with friends and other members of the congregation, saying, 'This is a symbol of the New Life.'

Activity – Easter Eggs

You need:

- hard-boiled eggs;
- new or very clean paint brushes;
- food colourings: cochineal, blue, green, yellow.

Children can paint their eggs at home using the brushes and food colouring. When they are dry, they can perhaps paint on some of the Easter symbols. Try to ensure that children don't see it as a competition.

At church the eggs can be laid on a table or cloth for the children themselves and for the whole congregation to see.

At the end of the service the children take their eggs and crack them, saying, 'This is a symbol of the New Life.'

Then they can eat them!

Rogationtide

Background

This was traditionally a time when Christians prayed for God's blessings on their crops and other aspects of their work on the land. A service was followed by a visit to various places in the neighbourhood. Often this was combined with 'The Beating of the Bounds', a very old custom from a time when it was important to know the boundaries of the parish. In many cases food and drink were supplied by the Church or wealthy people within the village.

George Herbert, the poet and country parson who lived in the seventeenth century, called this tradition 'Procession' and described it in the following terms:

The advantages of it are:

- first, a blessing of God for the fruits of the field;
- second, justice in the preservation of bounds;
- third, charity in loving walking and neighbourly accompanying one another, with reconciling differences at that time, if there be any;
- fourth, mercie in relieving the poor by a liberal distribution of alms.

Today

It is an opportunity to meet up with Christians who attend different services or another place of worship, or else people who do not regularly attend a place of worship.

We can combine prayer for God's blessing on our local environment and the fruitfulness of the earth with:

- prayer for God's kingdom coming and his will to be done;
- dedication of places, animals and objects to God (remembering that they are his already; it is our work with them that needs to be dedicated).

Practical points

- It is a good opportunity to make contact with local farmers; permission will be needed to walk over their land, and they can be invited to join in.
- If the service and walk are well publicized, many people who rarely come to a place of worship will join in.
- Refreshments or a picnic somewhere along the route are often included.
- With a combined benefice or in a rural circuit, it is a good idea to meet or walk on a common boundary. A friendly farmer might be prepared to provide transport for the less mobile with a tractor and trailer!
- Twelve different locations have been included, so everyone needs to choose the ones that are most appropriate.
- The style makes it possible for a number of different people to act as leader.
- Some locations will lend themselves to a circle dance (see page 165).
- Movement from place to place can be in the form of a procession with instruments, banners and singing.
- The sections can also be used on other occasions, for example as part of a service for children or for the environment as a whole.
- At some stage, a collection might be taken up for Christian Aid, since Christian Aid Week comes at Rogationtide.

....

1. At the place of worship

Hymn

'All people that on earth do dwell' (HO&N 21) *or*
'Joy to the world' (HO&N 370)

Prayer

We come before you, our God and Sustainer,
remembering that you are the Creator
and the source of all being.

Out of your love the universe was born.
From primordial darkness you put in place
all that is needed for life and growth
and saw that it was good . . .
You have put this world into our hands:
may we recognize your Spirit within it,
disturbing and challenging us to care for creation,
for the weak and the deprived.
Lord, we remember that we are called by you
to nourish the earth and its diversity of life,
to share the gifts you have given, with one another
and with the poor of the world. **Amen.**

or

Verses from Psalms 24, 50 and 104 (NIV, adapted)

The earth is the Lord's, and everything in it,
the world and all that live in it.
All the animals of the forest are the Lord's,
and so are the cattle upon a thousand hills.
The Lord makes grass grow for the cattle,
and plants for us to cultivate,
bringing forth food from the earth,
wine that gladdens our hearts,
oil to make our faces shine,
bread that sustains our hearts.
The Lord makes springs pour water into the valleys;
it flows between the mountains.
The birds of the air nest by the waters;
they sing among the branches.

Reading (Isaiah 55.12–56.1)

You will go out in joy and be led forth in peace; the mountains
and hills will burst into song before you, and all the trees of
the field will clap their hands. Instead of the thornbush will
grow the pine tree, and instead of briers the myrtle will grow.
This will be for the LORD's renown, for an everlasting sign,
which will not be destroyed. This is what the LORD says:
'Maintain justice and do what is right, for my salvation is close
at hand and my righteousness will soon be revealed.'

Acknowledgement and Forgiveness of Sins

We will present our failings, the damaged creation and the sufferings of ourselves and our animals to our Lord and Saviour Jesus Christ, who loves them and died for them as well as for us.

We will ask him to forgive and heal us; then we can go out to praise him and do his holy work in this community.

Dear Lord,
we are sorry for our failure to acknowledge that the creation
belongs to you, and we are responsible to you for its well-being.
Please forgive us for thoughts, words and actions unworthy of
sons and daughters of God, who are also brothers and sisters
of birds and beasts. Amen.

O Lord of life, forgive us all our offences and heal us.
Help us to love and to serve you through loving and serving
those around us, especially those we meet on this day's
journey. Give us the grace to cherish your whole creation,
from the lowliest to the highest part. Amen.

Procession to the Door

Let us now leave this place of worship, built to the glory of God;
let us go out into the glory of God's creation.
Let us seek for the wisdom to understand the rhythm of life,
our own rhythms and the rhythms of the earth;
to dance with the Spirit in the joy of God's creation.

Hymns

The following hymns have a number of verses, so the first verse can be sung at this point and further verses at the other locations. Instruments such as tambourines, cymbals and brass make a good accompaniment.

'When morning gilds the skies' (page 92)
'All creatures of our God and king' (HO&N 6)
'All things bright and beautiful' (HO&N 25)

'You shall go out with joy' (HO&N 766) (this has a single verse which will be repeated at each location)

Other hymns are suggested in the text, appropriate to one location.

2. At a meadow or pasture

Responses (if animals are present)

O let the works of the Lord
bless the Lord.
O let the beasts and cattle
bless the Lord.
O let all who care for God's world
bless the Lord.

(from the Benedicite)

or (if animals are not present, Psalm 23.1–3, NIV)

The LORD is my shepherd: I shall lack nothing.
He makes me lie down in green pastures,
he leads me beside quiet waters,
he restores my soul.
He guides me in paths of righteousness
for his name's sake.

Reading (Deuteronomy 11.13–15, NIV)

So if you faithfully obey the commands I am giving you today – to love the LORD your God and to serve him with all your heart and with all your soul – then I will send rain on your land in its season, both autumn and spring rains, so that you may gather in your grain, new wine and oil. I will provide grass in the fields for your cattle, and you will eat and be satisfied.

or (Psalm 147.7–11, authors' own translation)

> Sing to the Lord with thanksgiving;
> make music to our God on the harp.
> He veils the sky with clouds
> and provides the earth with rain
> and makes grass grow on the hills;
> he provides food for the cattle
> and for the young ravens when they call.
> He does not delight in the horse's strength,
> and he takes no pleasure in a runner's fleetness;
> the Lord delights in those who fear him,
> who put their hope in his unfailing love.

Prayers

For a meadow (to be mown for hay or silage)

> O God, who gave your servant Joseph the wisdom to plan
> ahead in time of plenty, bless these fields in their growing time
> and bless [the farmer's] [our] endeavours to conserve grass,
> so that your animals may have sufficient food for the winter,
> and praise you by their health and fertility until the spring
> comes once more. **Amen.**

For a pasture (with animals grazing)

> O Lord, who sends the rain and the sun so the grass may grow,
> giving food for your animals; bless these fields, that they may
> glorify you by giving abundant nourishment to the animals
> pastured here.
> Give us the love and wisdom to look after our animals, and
> through our care of the fields pass them on to the next
> generation in good heart, worthy of the trust you have placed
> in us. **Amen.**

Hymn

'The Lord my pasture shall prepare' (HO&N 653) *or*
'Loving Shepherd of thy sheep' (HO&N 434) (especially if
children are present)

3. At an orchard, fruit farm or vineyard

Opening Words

Praise be to you, my Lord, for our sister Mother Earth, who gives us her fruits in due season.

(St Francis of Assisi, *c.* 1181–1226)

Responses (based on Jeremiah 17.7–8)

Blessed are those who trust in the Lord;
they will be like trees planted by the water.
They do not fear when heat comes;
their leaves will be always green.
They have no worries in a year of drought;
and never fail to bear fruit.

Reading (John 15.1, 2, 5, NRSV)

I am the true vine and my Father is the vine-grower. He removes every branch in me that bears no fruit. Every branch that bears fruit he prunes to make it bear more fruit. I am the vine, you are the branches. Those who abide in me and I in them bear much fruit, because apart from me you can do nothing.

or (Luke 13.6–9, AV)

He spake also this parable; A certain man had a fig tree planted in his vineyard; and he came and sought fruit thereon, and found none. Then said he unto the dresser of his vineyard, Behold, these three years I come seeking fruit on this fig tree, and find none: cut it down; why cumbereth it the ground?

And he answering said unto him, Lord, let it alone this year also, till I shall dig about it, and dung it: And if it bear fruit, well: and if not, then after that thou shalt cut it down.

or

You often say, 'I would give, but only to the deserving'.
The trees in your orchard say not so, nor the flocks in your
      pasture.
They give that they may live, for to withhold is to perish.
There are those who give and know not pain in giving,
Nor do they seek joy, nor give with mindfulness of virtue.
They give as in yonder valley the myrtle breathes its fragrance
      into space.
Through the hands of such as these God speaks,
And from behind their eyes He smiles upon the earth.

(from Khalil Gibran, *The Prophet*)

Prayer

Father of all, whose first design for us was that we should live
in paradise in the garden of Eden, surrounded by trees of
many kinds; and who wonderfully restored us to grace by
means of the blood of your Son symbolized by fruit turned
into wine: we dedicate our work in this place to you.
Work with us, and bless us so that we may glorify you by
producing food for your children which is wholesome and
nourishing, and gives pleasure to those who partake of it;
thus may your kingdom come, and your will be done on earth,
as it is in heaven. **Amen.**

or

O Lord Jesus Christ, who at your last supper offered to your
heavenly Father the fruit made into wine, bless the fruit of
these trees, plants and bushes so that those who look after
them may be prayerful as they tend them, and ever mindful
of the great work you have done for us by means of your blood
shed on the cross. To you be glory and honour throughout all
ages. **Amen.**

Hymn

'For the fruits of his creation' (HO&N 185)

4. At a field of vegetables or roots

Reading: The Parable of the Different Soils (based on Matthew 13.1–9)

A farmer went out to sow his field. There was a footpath through it, too hard for the seed to take root, so it rotted or was eaten by the birds. Some of the ground was on rock with little depth of soil, so that the plants could not develop deep roots nor could the ground hold much moisture. The plants sprang up quickly but soon withered away. Some of the soil was deeper but impoverished so that it grew nettles, docks and thistles as well. The plants took root but the weeds grew more quickly so the plants were choked and died. But some soil was well tended and fertile, in good heart, and the seed that fell on it put down deep roots, grew tall and strong and yielded a rich harvest.

Responses

O Lord, save our hearts from being as the footpath,
too hard for your word to take root.
O Lord, save our hearts from being as the rocky ground,
where your word cannot be nourished and withers away.
O Lord, save us from being as the poor soil,
where your word is overpowered
by the cares and worries of our everyday life.
Bless us and make us fertile soil, in good heart,
where your word flourishes
and brings life to ourselves and to others. Amen.

Prayer

Lord God of all creation, we give you thanks for the plants which sustain and nourish both humans and animals. These humble vegetables and roots are full of good things to keep us and our animals in good health. Teach us about the importance of the humble things in life, and of humility in our own lives, following the example of our blessed Lord who in his great humility took our human flesh and lived on earth among us, and now reigns in glory. **Amen.**

Hymn

'He that is down need fear no fall' (page 94)

....

5. At a cornfield

Responses

As a man sows, so shall he reap.
Those who sow in tears shall reap in joy.
Except a grain of wheat fall into the ground and die,
it remains a single seed.
But if it dies, it produces many seeds,
And gives life to humankind and beast.
Lord, give us a good harvest
that your children may not go hungry.
But feed us also with yourself,
the true and eternal bread.

Reading (Isaiah 28.24–9, REB)

Will the ploughman spend his whole time ploughing,
breaking up his ground and harrowing it? Does he not, once
he has levelled it, broadcast the dill and scatter the cummin?
Does he not put in the wheat and barley in rows, and vetches
along the edge? Does not his God instruct him and train him
aright? . . . Grain is crushed, but not too long or too finely;
cartwheels rumble over it and thresh it, but they do not grind
it fine. Even this knowledge comes from the LORD of Hosts,
whose counsel is wonderful and whose wisdom is great.

Prayer

May the blessing of God be upon this field and on all the
cereal crops and cornfields of our countryside.
May they receive rain to swell the grain and sun to ripen it.
May the harvest be safely gathered in and stored.
May we see ourselves as harvesters for eternal life –
'For look! The fields are already ripe for harvest'. **Amen.**

Hymn

'God, whose farm is all creation' (HO&N 236) *or*
'I am the bread of life' (HO&N 299)

....

6. At a rural workshop or enterprise

Reading (Exodus 35.30–4, NIV)

The LORD has chosen Bezalel son of Uri, the son of Hur, of
the tribe of Judah, and he has filled him with the Spirit of
God, with skill, ability and knowledge in all kind of crafts – to
make artistic designs for work in gold, silver and bronze, to cut
and set stones, to work in wood and to engage in all kinds of
artistic craftsmanship. And [the Lord] has given both him and
Oholiab . . . the ability to teach others.

Prayer

O Creator God,
you work with us
in creating new things
from the materials you have given us
and you inspire us with skill and perseverance:
We glorify you,
because you made your children to be co-creators
and care about all that they make.

O Saviour of the world,
in whom all things were and are created,
you grieve with us over our failures
and your damaged creation:
We glorify you,
because you shed your blood on the cross
to reconcile all creation to the one who made it.

O Comforter Spirit,
you encourage us in the struggles of creating
and are always on our side:

We glorify you,
because your liberating power breathes through our world,
bringing new life to birth and overcoming evil.

or

Lord, for all who transform the raw materials
you have supplied:
Glory be to you.
Lord, for all who work with mind and eye
to design and to create:
Glory be to you.
Lord, for all who work with their hands
to shape and join and build:
Glory be to you.

Prayer

O Divine Creator,
we believe that you created human beings
in your own image as workers;
and we know that your Son, our Lord,
worked at Nazareth with his hands:
bless the hands that work here,
that in partnership with you,
they may create useful and beautiful things,
for the improvement of our human life and work,
and so glorify your holy name. **Amen.**

Hymn

'Forth in thy name' (HO&N 188) *or*
'Lord of all hopefulness' (HO&N 413)

7. At a wild or uncultivated place

Reading (Luke 12.24, 27, REB)

> Jesus said: 'Think of the ravens: they neither sow nor reap;
> they have no storehouse or barn; yet God feeds them. Think
> of the lilies: they neither spin nor weave; yet I tell you, even
> Solomon in all his splendour was not attired like one of them.'

Responses

> O all you green plants, shrubs and trees,
> O all you insects and creeping things,
> **Praise the Lord who made you and sustains you.**
> O all you birds and animals who hide yourselves,
> O all you stones and rocks, giving shelter,
> **Praise the Lord who made you and sustains you.**
> O heat and cold, rain and sun, dew and frost,
> O night and day, air and wind, summer and winter,
> **Praise the Lord who made you and sustains you.**

Poem: Wild Flowers

The old church stands down Old Church Lane, where it has
    stood for years.
It's seen the people come and go, their laughter and their tears.
It's hard to think that fine old church once colourful and new,
But long before the church was built, the wild flowers grew.

The village folk all gather down upon the village green,
To have a fête and celebrate, and crown the village queen.
To have a joke and have a laugh of how things used to be.
Village without the village folk, it wouldn't be the same.
But long before the village folk, the wild flowers came.

Lorries, heavy lorries all thunder through the lanes,
Revving up their engines and leaving diesel stains;
Tainting wayside verges, with tar and oil and grease,
Rumbling, shifting noises of now-forgotten peace.
But with the help of sunshine, and early morning rain,
The never failing cycle, wild flowers bloom again.

(Wilf Ward, 1948–)

Prayer

> We worship you, O Holy Spirit,
> whose creative power includes the wild and unknowable,
> reflecting the mystery and power of your Godhead.
> Help us to acknowledge and embrace
> our fear of what we do not know or understand,
> not to destroy but to protect the wild, free places of this
>   planet,
> so that we can save them for future generations.
> We praise you for their diversity and exuberance,
> and for their special place in your world.
> Breathe on us your grace and power
> so that like the wind we are free to go
> wherever you take us,
> not knowing where we come from
> or where we are going,
> but rejoicing in your wildness and your protection,
> who was sent as a companion for us
> by our Saviour and our Creator, one God,
> world without end. **Amen.**

Hymn

'There are hundreds of sparrows' (HO&N 890) *or*
'Who put the colours in the rainbow' (HO&N 915)

....

8. At a farmstead

Opening Words

Start outside the gate.

Leader   Peace be to this house and farm. (See Matthew 10.12)

Farmer   Grace and peace to you from God our Father and the
Lord Jesus Christ. (Romans 1.7, REB)

All   **Open for us the gates of righteousness;
we will enter and give thanks to the Lord.** (See Psalm
118.19)

Farmer (*opening gate*) This is the gate of the Lord through which
the righteous may enter. (See Psalm 118.20)

Reading (Deuteronomy 8.11–14, 17–18, NIV)

Be careful that you do not forget the LORD your God, failing to
observe his commands, his laws and his decrees . . . Otherwise,
when you eat and are satisfied, when you build fine houses and
settle down, and when your herds and flocks grow large . . .
and all you have is multiplied, then your heart will become
proud and you will forget the LORD your God, who brought you
out of Egypt, out of the land of slavery. You may say to yourself,
'My power and the strength of my hands have produced this
wealth for me.' But remember the LORD your God, for it is he
who gives you the ability to produce wealth, and so confirms his
covenant, which he swore to your forefathers . . .

or

Poem: A Winter Milking

All is quiet and dark but there is wakefulness:
The farmer pulls on his boots, the cows stir in their shed.
Light comes out of darkness, the machine springs into life.
The cows go swaying o'er the sanded yard,
Breath steaming, udders swinging,
Each in her place and known as she enters the parlour.
A trinity of creator, man and beast
Linked in the giving and receiving,
Held in God's heart but present here on earth.
Hear the gushing of the milk from willing teats,
The rhythmic, almost hypnotic pulsing of the milk along the line
Until it reaches the dairy and is discharged
Into the gently foaming, slowly chilling tank.
A procession of cows passes through the parlour,
The farmer knows which might have problems,
     might come bulling.
It is a world apart where on a good day
     all is harmony and pleasure.
The morning milking is the farmer's dawn prayer.

(Noël Lovatt)

Prayer

We thank you, heavenly Father,
for the hard work which takes place here,
and ask your blessing on the family
and on the whole enterprise.
We thank you for the working animal,
and for the machines
which take the toil out of our labour.

Keep all the food,
equipment and materials in this place
safe from disease, pollution and theft,
so that they may play their part
in bringing in a harvest,
to feed and clothe your world. **Amen.**

Responses

For the stirring of new life
throughout the countryside:
Thanks be to God.
For hard work with crops and animals
that both wearies and satisfies:
Thanks be to God.
For the security of a home
with warmth, food and family:
Thanks be to God.
Bless, O God, this house and farm
and those who live and work here.
Give them health and strength in their daily labours:
And thankfulness for all your gifts.

(Psalm 121.8, RSV)

The Lord keep your going out and your coming in:
from this time forth and for evermore. Amen.

Hymn

'For the beauty of the earth' (HO&N 184) *or*
'God whose farm is all creation' (HO&N 236)

9. At a place of hospitality

Reading

There was a very stately palace before him, the name of which was Beautiful, and it stood just by the highway-side. So I saw in my dream that he made haste and went forward, that if possible he might get lodging there, and went on till he came and stood before the gate where the porter was. Then said Christian to the porter, Sir, what house is this? and may I lodge here tonight? The porter answered, This house was built by the Lord of the hill and He built it for the relief and security of pilgrims. So Watchful, the porter, rang a bell, at the sound of which came out of the door of the house a grave and beautiful damsel, named Discretion, who ran to the door and called forth two or three more of the family; and many of them meeting him at the threshold of the house, said, Come in, thou blessed of the Lord. Then he bowed his head, and followed them into the house.

(from John Bunyan, *Pilgrim's Progress*)

Prayer

We thank you, Lord, that just as Martha and Mary
welcomed you into their home after your weary travelling,
so the people in this place of hospitality
welcome and look after those in need of rest and refreshment.
We bless you for their dedication and long hours of service,
and pray that you will strengthen and support them,
assuring them that in welcoming the stranger,
they are welcoming their Lord and Saviour, Jesus Christ.
Amen.

Hymn

'Fill thou my life' (HO&N 171) *or*
'From heaven you came' (HO&N 195)

10. At the village green

Opening Words (based on Psalm 133.1)

Behold, how good and joyful a thing it is:
Brothers and sisters, to dwell together in unity.

Reading (Matthew 25.34–40, NIV)

Then the King will say to those on his right, 'Come, you who
are blessed by my Father; take your inheritance, the kingdom
prepared for you since the creation of the world. For I was
hungry and you gave me something to eat, I was thirsty and
you gave me something to drink, I was a stranger and you
invited me in, I needed clothes and you clothed me, I was
sick and you looked after me, I was in prison and you came to
visit me.'

Then the righteous will answer him, 'Lord, when did we see
you hungry and feed you, or thirsty and give you something to
drink? When did we see you a stranger and invite you in, or
needing clothes and clothe you? When did we see you sick or
in prison and go to visit you?' The King will reply, 'I tell you
the truth, whatever you did for one of the least of these
brothers of mine, you did for me.'

Prayer

From petty feuds and jealousies,
from talking too much about our neighbours:
Good Lord, deliver us.
From forming into groups that exclude others,
from lack of proper trust and sharing:
Good Lord, deliver us.
For the pleasure of having friends nearby,
for the opportunities to plan and play together:
We thank you, Lord.
For those who spend their time and talents
to improve and beautify our surroundings:
We thank you, Lord.

or

O God, whose Son was content to share the life of Nazareth,
help us to bring his peace
into every house and every enterprise.
May we be good neighbours,
thinking more of what unites us than what separates us.
Give us the love to comfort the sorrowful
and offer help to those in trouble,
through your Son, our guide and pattern. **Amen.**

Hymn

'Bind us together, Lord' (HO&N 72) *or*
'Let there be love shared among us' (HO&N 386)

11. At a house or cottage

Reading (Matthew 7.24–7, authors' own version)

Everyone who hears my words and carries them out is like
someone building a house on a foundation of rock. The rain
came down, the streams rose, and the winds blew and beat
against that house, but it did not fall. Everyone who hears my
words and does not carry them out is like someone building
his house on sand. The rain came down, the streams rose, and
the winds blew and beat against that house, and it fell with a
great crash.

Prayers

May God bless *this* house and those living in it;
**May all the loving here
be as strong as a house built upon rock,
withstanding the storms of life.**

May God bless *all* our houses and those *who* live in them;
**May all our loving there
be as strong as a house built upon rock,
withstanding the storms of life.**

May the Lord be praised for the animals
who share our homes and lives.
**We thank you, Lord, for designing a world
in which animals can live with us
and be our companions.
Help us to care for them,
remembering that you made them
and delight in them. Amen.**

Prayer

Father in heaven,
whose Son came to earth
and lived in a human family,
we thank you for the blessings
of life together and the gift of children.
Teach us to live in harmony,
listening to the needs and views of others.
May your name be kept holy
and your will be done
in the small everyday things of life,
so that your kingdom is built in our homes,
through Jesus Christ our Lord. **Amen.**

Hymn

'Rock of ages' (HO&N 584) *or*
'Little drops of water' (page 94)

....

12. In a garden

Reading (verses from Genesis 2, authors' own version)

The LORD God planted a garden in Eden, in the east, and
there he put the human being, whom he had formed, to till it
and to keep it. And the LORD God walked in the garden at the
time of the evening breeze.

or (Luke 23.42–3, NRSV, adapted)

> One of the criminals who was crucified with him said: 'Jesus, remember me when you come into your kingdom.' Jesus replied: 'Truly I tell you, today you will be with me in the Heavenly Garden.'*

Responses

God has made so many different kinds of plants for gardens.
God has made so many different kinds of people for his world.
Some plants need to be in the sun; some like to be in the shade.
Some of us need to be at the centre; some of us are retiring.
Some plants hug the ground and others reach for the sky.
Some of us have a lowly role in life and others have great ambitions.
Some plants grow in rich soil
and bring forth flowers, seeds and fruits in abundance.
Some of us are full-nourished
and produce marvellous ideas or creations that enrich the lives of all.
Some plants do best in poor soil but it takes all their strength to survive.
Some of us are so straitened in our lives that survival is our only achievement.

Prayer

O Lord, we need to accept
that you made us all so different,
with our own temperaments and talents.
Like plants, we cannot change our nature,
yet you rejoice in each one of us being special.
Help us come to terms with who we are
and what we are called upon to do;
wherever our lives are planted,
grant that we may praise you and glorify your name. **Amen.**

---

* 'Paradise' comes from a Persian word meaning 'pleasure garden'.

or

We thank you, heavenly Father,
for this beautiful garden,
and for all the loving work that has made it so.

Bless this garden,
so that through its peace and beauty
we may find a place of
refreshment in a busy world.

We praise you for the wildlife,
the small, hidden creatures,
the bees gathering nectar,
the singing birds, the busy insects.

Help us to be generous,
sharing the abundance that you give.
May all your creatures here live in peace with one another,
in accordance with your design and our future hope,
through Jesus Christ our Lord. **Amen.**

Hymn

'For the beauty of the earth' (HO&N 184) *or*
'God whose farm is all creation' (HO&N 236) *or*
'Morning has broken' (HO&N 450) *or*
'Lord Jesus hath a garden' (OB 105)

Readings for a wild or uncultivated place

O ancient forest of life
A fairie lace, silvery green
Festoons the grey, lichened boughs
Gossamer curtains of intricate weave
Eerie and silent in the mist-laden air.
Gnarled, distorted limbs reach out to the sky
Twisted and torn by countless winds and storms
Into grotesque, unnatural shapes;
While your strong sturdy trunks
Send down their life-giving roots into

The darkness of that rich, black primordial earth
Fed over aeons of time with the bodies of
Those gone before, and
Watered by the grey, cold waters of the loch
That tosses and surges, or
Lies quiet and silent
At the whim of the winds.
If only we could recognize the knowledge
Of your countless years,
Could know the things you've seen
Maybe then humankind
Could learn your secrets
And respect you
O ancient forest of life.

(Linda J. Probyn)

This reading speaks of recognizing God in holy places that are part of the 'otherness':

> On either side of them, as they glided onwards, the rich meadow grass seemed that morning of a freshness and a greenness unsurpassable. Never had they noticed the roses so vivid, the willow-herb so riotous, the meadow-sweet so odorous and pervading. Then the murmur of the approaching weir began to hold the air, and they felt a consciousness that they were nearing the end, whatever that might be, that surely awaited their expedition.

> A wide half-circle of foam and glinting lights and shining shoulders of green water, the great weir closed the backwater from bank to bank, troubled all the quiet surface with twirling eddies and floating foam-streaks, and deadened all other sounds with its solemn and soothing rumble. In midmost of the stream, embraced in the weir's shimmering arm-spread, a small island lay anchored, fringed close with willow and silver birch and alder. Reserved, shy, but full of significance, it hid whatever it might hold behind a veil, keeping it till the hour should come and with the hour, those who were called and chosen.

> Slowly, but with no doubt or hesitation whatever, and in something of a solemn expectancy, the two passed through the

broken, tumultuous water and moored their boat at the flowery margin of the island. In silence they landed and pushed through the blossom and scented herbage and undergrowth that led up to the level ground, till they stood on a little lawn of a marvellous green, set round with Nature's own orchard trees – crab-apple, wild cherry, and sloe.

'This is the place of my song-dream, the place the music played to me,' whispered the Rat, as if in a trance, 'Here, in this holy place, here if anywhere, surely we shall find Him!'

Then suddenly the Mole felt a great Awe fall upon him, an awe that turned his muscles to water, bowed his head, and rooted his feet to the ground.

(from Kenneth Grahame, *The Wind in the Willows*)

Hymns

When morning gilds the skies

When morning gilds the skies,
My heart awaking cries,
May Jesus Christ be praised:
Alike at work and prayer
To Jesus I repair;
May Jesus Christ be praised.

Whene'er the sweet church bell
Sounds over hill and dell,
May Jesus Christ be praised:
O hark to what it sings,
As joyously it rings,
May Jesus Christ be praised.

Let earth's wide circle round
In joyful notes resound,
May Jesus Christ be praised:
Let air, and sea, and sky
From depth to height reply,
May Jesus Christ be praised.

Be this while life is mine,
My canticle divine,
May Jesus Christ be praised:
Be this the eternal song
Through all the ages on,
May Jesus Christ be praised.

('Laudes Domini'; NEH 473; metre 666 D)

Some or all of the following verses can be used if a verse is being
sung at each location, with verse 4 above being the last verse.

Does sadness fill my mind?
A solace here I find,
May Jesus Christ be praised:
When evil thoughts molest,
With this I shield my breast,
May Jesus Christ be praised.

Be this, when day is past,
Of all my thoughts the last,
May Jesus Christ be praised:
The night becomes as day,
When from the heart we say,
May Jesus Christ be praised.

My tongue will never tire
Of chanting with the choir,
May Jesus Christ be praised:
This song of sacred joy,
It never seems to cloy,
May Jesus Christ be praised.

To God, the Word, on high
The hosts of angels cry,
May Jesus Christ be praised:
Let mortals, too, upraise
Their voice in hymns of praise,
May Jesus Christ be praised.

He that is down needs fear no fall

He that is down needs fear no fall,
He that is low no pride;
He that is humble ever shall
Have God to be his guide.

I am content with what I have,
Little be it or much;
And, Lord, contentment still I crave,
Because thou savest such.

Fullness to such a burden is
That go on pilgrimage;
Here little, and hereafter bliss,
Is best from age to age.

(John Bunyan, 1628–88; CM)
Tune: York

Little drops of water

Little drops of water,
Little grains of sand
Make the mighty ocean
And the beauteous land.

And the little moments,
Humble though they be,
Make the mighty ages
Of eternity.

Little deeds of kindness,
Little words of love
Make our earth an Eden,
Like the heaven above.

Little seeds of mercy,
Sown by humble hands,
Grow to bless the people
In this and many lands.

Glory, then, for ever
Be to God on high,
Beautiful and loving,
To eternity.

(Mrs J. A. Carney, 1845; metre 6 5 6 5)
Tune: Gott ein Vater

SUMMER

Trinity

Background

The Sunday after Pentecost was not observed as a separate feast in honour of the Trinity until the fourteenth century. It became very popular in this country, but does not seem to have been marked by any particular ceremonies. After the dramatic events of Pentecost, Trinity Sunday can pass very quietly. Yet the belief in the Trinity, the Three in One, is one of the basic tenets of the Christian creed, giving us a God who can be described as Love in Action, source of all human love, or as the Divine Community, pattern for all human communities. Rather than a complete service, prayers from different sources are offered, together with a playlet for children.

Praises and prayers

God is the Three in One

God is the Trinity and God is the Unity;
God is all our life: nature, mercy and grace.
God is the one who makes us to love,
and the endless fulfilling of all true desires.

(Julian of Norwich)

Praise to God

Praise him in his glory, heaven and earth,
and every creature that is in heaven and on the earth
and under the earth, and such as are on the seas
and all that are in them.
Let us praise and glorify him for ever.
Glory to the Father, and to the Son and to the Holy Spirit.
Let us praise and glorify him for ever.

(St Francis)

Glory to God

Glory to the Father, the God of love, who created us;
who continually preserves and sustains us;
who has loved us with an everlasting love,
and given us the light of the knowledge of his glory
in the face of Jesus Christ.
Blessed be God for ever.

Glory to Jesus Christ our Lord.
Though he was rich, yet for our sake he became poor;
he was tested in every way as we are, yet without sin;
he proclaimed the good news of the kingdom,
and was obedient even to the point of death, death on a cross.
He was raised from the dead and is alive for ever,
and has opened the kingdom of heaven to all who trust in
    him.
He is seated at God's right hand in the Father's glory;
he will come to be our judge.
Blessed be God for ever.

Glory to the Holy Spirit, the Lord, the giver of life,
by whom we are born into the family of God,
and made members of the body of Christ;
whose witness confirms us; whose wisdom teaches us;
whose power enables us; who will do for us
    more than we can ask or think.
Blessed be God for ever.

(from the *Methodist Covenant Service*)

Prayers

Holy God, Creator of all,
Your righteousness and justice
Transcend our wildest imaginings.
Your Power threw the stars into the void;
It cradles the most delicate of flowers.
In your image you created humanity,
You set us in the midst of the wonder and beauty
    of your creation,
A creation which we have abused and marred –

Forgive us for our failure to live up to the trust you have
   placed in us.

Holy God, Redeemer of all,
You came to us as the Christ
And in the Power of your eternal love.
Long ago in Bethlehem you came;
With humility and love you stood
In the doorway between two worlds –
Bid us to be transformed,
To become one with you.
In our fear we ran from you;
In our fear and dread of change
We killed you.
Loving Lord Jesus, forgive our fear.

Holy God, Sustainer of life,
Eternal Spirit of creativity and wisdom,
In your Power you dwell in each and every one of us.
In the humility and in the awesomeness of your love,
You give to us the gift of eternal life.
In our greed and our selfishness
Too often we refuse to listen;
Too often we turn away from the blinding light.
Too often we reject you.
Holy Spirit of Wisdom and Mercy,
forgive us for turning away
from the knowledge of your love.

Holy Trinity of Creation, Love and Wisdom,
Come, live and dwell in us today;
Create in us your perfect dwelling place in the world.
Blessed be God, the Three in One and One in Three.
Blessed be God, Creator, Redeemer and Sustainer.
Blessed be God for ever. Amen.

(Linda J. Probyn)

Trinity Triads

Power of all powers
We worship you.
Light of all lights
We worship you.
Life of all lives
We worship you.

Source of all life
We turn to you.
Saviour of all life
We turn to you.
Sustainer of all life
We turn to you.

Ground of all being
We rest in you.
Salt of all being
We rest in you.
Unity of all being
We rest in you.

Maker of all creatures
We honour you.
Friend of all creatures
We honour you.
Force of all creatures
We honour you.

Love before time
We adore you.
Love in dark time
We adore you.
Love in present time
We adore you.

(from Ray Simpson, *Celtic Worship Through the Year*)

The shield of the Father

The shield of the Father,
Covering, caring,
From evil's snaring.

The shield of the Son,
New life supplying
Defence against dying.

The shield of the Spirit,
A shelter discover,
Where we can recover.

The shield of the Three
For body and soul;
The shield of the Three
Keeping us whole.

(from David Adam, *Tides and Seasons*)

Affirmation of Faith

We believe in God above us;
making and sustaining life,
sending sun and gentle rainfall,
blessing land and guiding us.

We believe in God beside us,
Jesus, with us as we labour,
suffering for his hurt creation,
dying for us on the cross,
rising to bring life to us,
Saviour of the natural world.

We believe in God within us,
Holy Spirit, breath of God.
Bringing life to all creation,
Our companion and our guide.

We believe in God around us
Father, Son and Holy Spirit
Lord of us and Lord of nature
sharing blessing, peace and love. **Amen.**

Blessing

The Creator who brought order out of chaos,
give peace to you.
The Saviour who stilled the raging storm,
give peace to you.
The Spirit who broods on the deeps,
give peace to you.

(from David Adam, *The Open Gate*)

Clover leaf

Background

A favourite way of talking about the Trinity is to compare it to a
clover leaf with its three essential parts making up the whole. The
following is a humble attempt to turn this image into picture and
language, in such a way that it can be performed by children. It
has been done in a spirit of reverence and we hope that it will not
be seen as trivializing this great mystery.

Preparation

You need three children to be Clover Leaves 1, 2 and 3, then a
chorus of younger children, and the Leader who can be an adult.

Make three cardboard leaves about 2ft × 1ft (60cm × 30cm), the
same shape as clover leaves, with a pointed bit where the stalk
fastens. Each one needs a 'stalk' made out of string or ribbon.
Seeing that they represent the three persons of the Trinity, it's
probably best if they are different in some way, perhaps three
shades of green, or one plain green and the other two patterned
but differently. See the endnote on page 104 for some
information about clover.

Clover Leaf 1 comes on, carrying one leaf.

CL1	Hello, everyone!
	I'm a very important person.
	When I grow in your field,
	the grass is longer and lusher
	because I feed it with my goodness.
	My name is Clover Leaf.
Group	**Oh no it's not!**
CL1	Oh yes it is!
Group	**Oh no it's not!**
Leader	They're right you know;
	you're *not* Clover Leaf, full stop –
	you're only a *part* of Clover Leaf.
	Where are the other parts?

Clover Leaf 2 comes on, carrying one leaf.

CL2	Here I am. Sorry I'm late.

Turns to face CL1 and they whisper together, then turn and face front.

CL1, 2	Hello everyone!
	We're very important people.
	When we grow in your fields
	the grass is longer and lusher
	because we feed it with our goodness.
	Our name is Clover Leaf.
Group	**Oh no it's not!**
CL1, 2	Oh yes it is!
Group	**Oh no it's not!**
Leader	They're right you know;
	you're *not* Clover Leaf, full stop –
	you're only a *part* of Clover Leaf.
	Where is the third part?

Clover Leaf 3 comes on, carrying one leaf.

CL3	Here I am. Sorry I'm late.

Whispers to the others and then they all stand in a row, holding up their leaves with the stalks coming straight down.

CL1, 2, 3	Hello everyone! We're very important people. When we grow in your fields, the grass is longer and lusher because we feed it with our goodness. Our name is Clover Leaf.
Group	**Oh no it's not!**
CL1, 2, 3	Oh yes it is!
Group	**Oh no it's not!**
Leader	They're right you know; you're *not* Clover Leaf, not properly; you're just three bits – you're not joined together in any way.

CL1, 2 and 3 turn to face each other and whisper, then all stand in a row again, holding up their leaves sideways so that the stalk of one touches the leaf of the next.

Leader	Hey wait, you're still not a proper clover leaf.
CL1, 2 , 3	Oh yes we are!
Group	**Oh no you're not!**
CL1, 2, 3	But we're joined together, like you said.
Leader	But you're not joined together properly.

They turn to face each other and whisper, then all stand in a row again, holding up their leaves so they are all touching, but two are pointing downwards and one is pointing upwards.

Leader	I don't believe it! You're still not a proper clover leaf. You need to put your leaves together so that the three stalks touch, then there is one complete leaf on one stalk and the stalk goes down into the ground. Only then do you become complete, only then can you do your job in the fields.

They turn to face each other and whisper, then they all stand in a row again, holding up their leaves so that there is one leaf at the top pointing downwards and two out sideways, and the three stalks touch each other and look like one stalk going down to the ground.

Leader   Well done, you've got it right at last.
We can see that each of you
is an important part of the whole,
but you're not the whole clover leaf
until you come together in this way.

CL1, 2, 3   Hello, everyone! We're very important people.
When we grow in your fields,
the grass is longer and lusher
because we feed it with our goodness.
Our name is Clover Leaf.

We also have another important job
and that's to help people understand
what God is like.
God has three parts, just like us
but they are all joined together
to be the one God, Father, Son and Holy Spirit,
as it says in the hymn
which we're all going to sing now.

Hymn

'Three in one and one in three' (HO&N 685)

Endnote

Clover is a remarkable plant in that it can fix nitrogen from the air. Farmers with low fertilizer usage can obtain all the nitrogen needed through sowing clover in the sward, resulting in lower costs and improved pasture.

A Celebration of God's World in Summer

Background

This service is based on the hymn 'All things bright and beautiful'. It is suitable for all ages and for a town, suburban or country setting. The biblical quotations at the beginning of each theme can be said by children, either as a group or as individuals. The longer pieces can be said each by a different worshipper.

Preparation

Find a visual focus for each theme. Here are some suggestions:

Theme 1: a flowering plant or a vase of flowers is brought up by a child.

Theme 2: a tame bird or picture of a bird is brought up by a bird-watcher or fancier (a recording of birdsong can also be played).

Theme 3: a small tree is brought up by a forester or owner of a nursery.

Theme 4: a bowl of strawberries, or other fruit in season, is brought up by a keen gardener or owner of a 'pick-your-own' business.

Theme 5: a painting of a sunset is brought up by a local artist if possible.

Place a table at the front, covering it with green material or crêpe paper, and arrange for children to decorate it.

....

Welcome

Hymn

'All things bright and beautiful' (HO&N 25)

....

Theme 1: Each little flower that opens

Opening Words (Matthew 6.28–9, NRSV)

> Consider the lilies of the field, how they grow;
> they neither toil nor spin;
> yet I tell you, even Solomon in all his glory
> was not clothed like one of these.

A short silence while the plant or vase of flowers is brought up.

Reading

> Flowers preach to us if we will hear.
> The rose saith in the dewy morn:
> I am most fair;
> Yet all my loveliness is born
> Upon a thorn.
> The lilies say: Behold how we
> Preach without words of purity.
> The violets whisper from the shade:
> Men scent our fragrance on the air
> Yet take no heed
> Of humble lessons we would read.
> The merest grass
> Alongside the roadside where we pass
> Tells of his love who sends the dew,
> Who sends the rain and sunshine too.

> (from Christina Rossetti, 'Consider the Lilies of the Field')

Hymn

'Jesus is Lord! Creation's voice proclaims it' (HO&N 352)

Theme 2: Each little bird that sings

Opening Words (Matthew 6.26, NRSV)

> Look at the birds of the air: they neither sow
> nor reap nor gather into barns
> and yet your heavenly Father feeds them.
> Not one [sparrow] will fall to the ground
> unperceived by your Father.

A short silence while the bird or picture is brought up.

Poem: To a Skylark

Ethereal minstrel! pilgrim of the sky!
Dost thou despise the earth where cares abound?
Or, while the wings aspire, are heart and eye
Both with thy nest upon the dewy ground?
Thy nest which thou canst drop into at will,
Those quivering wings composed, that music still!

To the last point of vision and beyond
Mount, daring Warbler! that love-prompted strain
('Twixt thee and thine a never-failing bond)
Thrills not the less the bosom of the plain.
Yet might'st thou seem, proud privilege!, to sing
All independent of the leafy spring.

Leave to the nightingale her shady wood;
A privacy of glorious light is thine;
Whence thou dost pour upon the world a flood
Of harmony, with instinct more divine;
Type of the wise who soar, but never roam,
True to the kindred points of Heaven and Home!

(William Wordsworth, 1770–1850)

Hymn

'Sing to God new songs of worship' (HO&N 603)

Theme 3: The ripe fruits in the garden

Opening Words (based on verses from Genesis 2)

> The Lord God planted a garden in Eden
> And there he placed the human being he had formed.
> And the Lord God placed the human being in the garden
> To tend it and to care for it.

A short silence while the bowl of fruit is brought up.

Reading

> Our England is a garden, and such gardens are not made
> By singing 'Oh, how beautiful' and sitting in the shade,
> While better men than we go out and start their working lives
> At grubbing weeds from gravel-paths with broken dinner
>   knives.
>
> There's not a pair of legs so thin, there's not a head so thick,
> There's not a hand so weak and white, nor yet a heart so sick,
> But it can find some needful job that's crying to be done,
> For the Glory of the Garden glorifieth every one.
>
> Then seek your job with thankfulness and work till further
>   orders,
> If it's only netting strawberries or killing slugs on borders;
> And when your back stops aching and your hands begin to
>   harden,
> You will find yourself a partner in the Glory of the Garden.
>
> Oh, Adam was a gardener, and the God who made him sees
> That half a proper gardener's work is done upon his knees,
> So when your work is finished, you can wash your hands and
>   pray
> For the Glory of the Garden, that it may not pass away!
> And the Glory of the Garden, it shall never pass away!

(from Rudyard Kipling, 'The Glory of the Garden')

Hymn

'For the fruits of his creation' (HO&N 185)

Theme 4: The tall trees in the greenwood

Opening Words (based on Psalm 1.3–4)

> The righteous are like trees planted along a river bank
> Which yield their fruit in due season:
> Their leaves shall never wither
> And they shall prosper in all they do.

A short silence while the tree is brought up.

Reading: A Tree

> A tree grows, bears fruit – then, after a certain time, it no
> longer grows, it loses its leaves, its branches wither. What
> happens? Why is its vital energy checked? Because it did not
> sink deep enough roots into the earth on which it stands.
> Anyone who has to do with trees knows what I mean. The
> same thing, I thought to myself, has happened with us
> humans. Humanity has not had deep enough roots. It has not
> found sustenance and fresh impetus, because the ethical code
> on which it was based was too narrow and did not have a deep
> foundation. It has concerned itself only with human beings
> and our relations with human beings. It has given only a
> passing nod to our relationship with other living creatures,
> looking upon it as a nice bit of sentimentality, quite innocuous
> but of no great significance. For only if we have an ethical
> attitude in our thinking about all living creatures does our
> humanity have deep roots and a rich flowering that cannot
> wither.

> (Albert Schweitzer, 1875–1965)

Hymn

'O Lord my God' (HO&N 511)

Theme 5: The sunset and the morning

Opening Words (based on verses from Genesis 1 and Psalm 19)

> God made two great lights:
> The greater to rule the day and the lesser to rule the night;
> The sun comes forth as a bridegroom from his chamber
> And like a strong man runs his course with joy.

A short silence while the picture is brought up.

Poem: The Setting Sun

This scene, how beauteous to a musing mind,
That now swift slides from my enchanted view;
The sun sweet-setting yon far hills behind,
In other worlds his visits to renew:
What spangled glories all round him shine;
What nameless colours, cloudless and serene
(A heav'nly prospect, brightest in decline)
Attend his exit from this lovely scene.

So sets the Christian's sun, in glories clear:
So shines his soul at his departure here:
No clouding doubts, nor misty fears arise,
To dim hope's golden rays of being forgiven;
His sun sweet-setting in the clearest skies,
In faith's assurance wings the soul to heaven.

(John Clare, 1793–1864)

Hymn

'The day thou gavest, Lord, is ended' (HO&N 638) *or*
'Yes, God is good' (see p. 114)

Theme 6: The Lord God made them all

Opening Words (based on verses from Genesis 1 and 2)

God saw all that he had made
And it was very good.
On the sixth day God completed all his work,
Heaven and earth with all their mighty throng,
And God blessed the seventh day and made it holy.
Because on the seventh day he rested from all his work.

A short silence to contemplate the assembled gifts.

Poem: When the Time Was Right
(This requires several voices, preferably young people's voices)

God looked into space
but nothing was around:
just darkness and wind,
not a smell, sight or sound.
Then God said to himself,
'I think we'll have light',
so the darkness stopped
when the time was right.

God made the night and day,
but they weren't the same.
Then he made sea and sky
and he gave each their name;
and when God saw the ocean,
which was sparkling and bright,
he was glad he'd made water
when the time was right.

God said to himself,
'Now I'd like to see land.
I'd like meadows and mountains
and shores full of sand.'
So he brought earth from water
and was pleased with the sight
of the plants which all grew
when the time was right.

Then God looked at the sky
and he found it too plain.
It was all coloured blue
and was filled up with rain.
So he made sun and moon
to change day into night
and the stars blinked their eyes
when the time was right.

God looked at the land
and decided, one day,
to put fish in the sea
and make sure that they'd stay.
He put birds in the air
and they all shook with fright
till God taught them to fly
when the time was right.

Then God made the animals,
some small and some large,
and soon he was asking,
'Who on earth will take charge?'
So he waited and wondered,
till with careful insight,
he made man and made woman
when the time was right.

Then God watched from a distance
to see what they'd do
with the world and its creatures
and with each other too.
Sometimes they forgot
what God wanted or said,
then they'd go their own way
and do their will instead.

And it hurt God that people
whom he'd made out of love
should forget how to live,
what to say, where to move.
Should he punish and hate them?
Should he leave them to fight?
No! He sent to them Jesus
when the time was right.
When the time was right.

(from John L. Bell, *He Was in the World*)

Hymn

'Great is thy faithfulness '(HO&N 249)

Prayers

Blessing

> May God the Creator,
> who made us and all living things
> and all the marvels
> which surround us in the natural world,
> bless us, our homes and our families,
> now and for ever. **Amen.**

Final Hymn

'You shall go out with joy' (HO&N 766)
or 'Yes, God is good' (see p. 114)

Hymn

Yes, God is good

Yes, God is good – in earth and sky,
from ocean depths and spreading wood,
ten thousand voices seem to cry:
God made us all, and God is good.

The sun that keeps his trackless way,
and downward pours his golden flood,
night's sparkling hosts, all seem to say
in accents clear that God is good.

The joyful birds prolong the strain,
their song with every spring renewed;
the air we breathe, and falling rain,
each softly whispers: God is good.

I hear it in the rushing breeze;
the hills that have for ages stood,
the echoing sky and roaring seas,
all swell the chorus: God is good.

Yes, God is good, all nature says,
by God's own hand with speech endued;
and man, in louder notes of praise,
should sing for joy that God is good.

For all Your gifts we bless You, Lord,
but chiefly for our heavenly food,
Your pardoning grace, Your quickening word,
these prompt our song, that God is good.

(John Hampden Gurney, 1802–62; metre 86 86)
Tune: Williams

Lammastide

Background

Lammastide corresponds to the Hebrew Feast of Weeks when a sheaf of the first of the barley harvest was offered (Leviticus 23.9ff., Numbers 28.26–31, Deuteronomy 16.10, 16) and Lammas Day itself is 1 August. The word 'Lammas' first appears in the writings of King Alfred and is thought to be derived from an English word for 'loaf' followed by 'mass'. In the early English Church it was customary to consecrate bread made from the first-ripe corn on this day, probably in thanksgiving for the harvest.

Today

It is not easy to celebrate in the traditional way, by bringing in a sheaf of corn and a loaf baked by the local baker, but the offering of these is still included in the following service. However, the service could also take place without this section or with a loaf (baked from local flour if possible) offered by the person who has baked it.

Hymn

'Praise and thanksgiving, Father, we offer' (HO&N 558) *or*
'O worship the King' (HO&N 551) *or*
'Eat this bread' (Taizé; CG 31)

Old Testament Reading (Deuteronomy 26.1–4, NIV)

When you have entered the land that the Lord your God is giving you as an inheritance and have taken possession of it and settled in it, take some of the firstfruits of all that you produce from the soil of the land and put them in a basket. Then go to the place that the Lord your God will choose as a dwelling for his Name and say to the priest in office at the time, 'I declare today to the Lord your God that I have come to the land that the Lord swore to our ancestors to give us.'

Psalm (based on Psalm 65)

O God of our salvation,
in whom all put their trust,
you established the mountains by your power,
you silence the roaring of the seas.
You care for the land and water it;
you enrich it abundantly.
The streams of God are filled with water
to provide the people with corn.
You drench its furrows and level its ridges;
you soften it with showers and bless its crops.
You crown the year with your bounty,
the grasslands of the desert overflow.
The hills are clothed with gladness,
and the meadows are covered with flocks.
The valleys are mantled with corn
so that they shout for joy and sing.

New Testament Reading (John 6.5–12, NIV)

When Jesus looked up and saw a great crowd coming towards him, he said to Philip, 'Where shall we buy bread for these people to eat?' He asked this only to test him, for he already had in mind what he was going to do. Philip answered him, 'Eight months' wages would not buy enough bread for each one to have a bite!' Another of his disciples, Andrew, Simon Peter's brother, spoke up, 'Here is a boy with five small barley loaves and two small fish, but how far will they go among so many?' Jesus said, 'Make the people sit down.' There was plenty of grass in that place, and the men sat down, about five thousand of them. Jesus then took the loaves, gave thanks, and distributed to those who were seated as much as they wanted. He did the same with the fish. When they had all had enough to eat, he said to the disciples, 'Gather the pieces that are left over. Let nothing be wasted.'

or (2 Corinthians 9.6–11, REB)

Remember: sow sparingly, and you will reap sparingly; sow bountifully, and you will reap bountifully. Each person should give as he has decided for himself; there should be no reluctance, no sense of compulsion; God loves a cheerful giver. And it is in God's power to provide you with all good gifts in abundance, so that, with every need always met to the full, you may have something to spare for every good cause; as scripture says: '[God] lavishes his gifts on the needy; his benevolence lasts for ever.' Now he who provides seed for sowing and bread for food will provide the seed for you to sow; he will multiply it and swell the harvest of your benevolence, and you will always be rich enough to be generous. Through our action such generosity will issue in thanksgiving to God.

The congregation stands.

1st Speaker	Let us praise God:
	for the rich soil of the countryside,
	and drills drawn straight across the field;
	for the green corn springing out of the earth,
	and the warm sweetness of the rain:
	Let us praise God.
	For the power of tractors
	and for all the machines that ease our labour;
	and for the skill of those who gather the harvest:
	Let us praise God.
2nd Speaker	Let us praise God:
	for all who work on the farm and in the field;
	for their hope and courage
	in days of difficulty and disappointment:
	Let us praise God.
	For those who, often unnoticed and unsung,
	provide their fellow-citizens with the means of life,
	for the salvation of town and country:
	Let us praise God.

3rd Speaker	For all who take the true craftsman's pride in the work they do, and know the satisfaction that comes from a hard day's work well done: **Let us praise God.** For the bread given us as our daily food, and for that Bread of Life which we receive at the Lord's table: **Let us praise God.**
All sing	**Praise God, from whom all blessings flow, Praise him, all creatures here below. Praise him above, Angelic host, Praise Father, Son, and Holy Ghost.**

Hymn

'Bread of the world in mercy broken' (HO&N 83) *or*
'I am the bread of life' (HO&N 299)

Offering of Grain and Bread

A farmer and a baker or farmer's wife come up during the hymn carrying a sheaf of corn and a loaf of bread. They may be followed by other farmers, family members, farm workers or members of Young Farmers' clubs.

Farmer	In the name of the farmers and farm workers of our community, I bring this sheaf of corn, the first-fruits of our harvest. We offer it to Almighty God and pray for his blessing on the ingathering of all our crops.

The farmer presents the sheaf at the altar table.

Baker or farmer's wife	In the name of the people of our community, I bring this loaf made from the first ears of the ripe corn. We offer it to God, and pray for his blessing on our homes and our families, on the food we eat and the work we do, and on all the daily life of our village.

The baker or farmer's wife presents the loaf at the altar table.

All   **All things come from you,**
             and of your own have we given you.

Leader   The Lord be with you.
All   **And also with you.**
Leader   Lift up your hearts.
All   **We lift them to the Lord.**
Leader   Let us give thanks to the Lord our God.
All   **It is right to give thanks and praise.**
Leader   It is indeed right, it is our duty and our joy,
             that we should at all times and in all places,
             give you thanks and praise,
             eternal God, through Jesus Christ your Son.
             We thank you because you have set us
             in the midst of your bounteous creation
             and called us to be fellow-workers with you;
             we thank you because you have ripened our first-fruits
             with the rain of heaven, and the warmth of the sun.
All   **Glory be to you, O Lord most high. Amen.**

Leader   Let us pray.

Prayer

             O God, who has made heaven and earth,
             and all that is in them,
             we pray you to bless these first-fruits of harvest
             and to multiply them abundantly.
             We pray for seasonable weather
             that this year's harvest may be a plentiful one.
             Rejoicing in your gifts, may we offer our thanks
             to your divine Majesty, through Jesus Christ our Lord.
             Amen.

or

             O God, whose Son blessed the loaves
             that were brought to him:
             bless this bread made from your gift in creation,

that those who live nearby and those who live far off
may share in your bounty
and find health for body, mind and spirit.
Through the same Jesus Christ our Lord,
who is the true bread which comes down from heaven
and gives life and salvation to the world. **Amen.**

**The grace of our Lord Jesus Christ,
and the love of God,
and the fellowship of the Holy Spirit,
be with us all evermore. Amen.**

All return to their seats.

An Address or Talk may be given.

Hymn

'To Thee, O Lord, our hearts we raise' (HO&N 696) *or*
'We plough the fields and scatter' (HO&N 719) *or*
'You shall go out with joy' (HO&N 766)

Blessing

AUTUMN

Harvest

Background

Harvest has surely been celebrated ever since human beings first planted seeds, cut the heads of grain and stored them to use through the times of scarcity. Coming closer to our own time, when the children of Israel entered the Promised Land, they adapted the agricultural festivals being kept there and these have come down to us today: Lammas, the time of the first-fruits, corresponds to the Feast of Weeks when the first sheaf of the barley harvest was offered; our Harvest Festival corresponds to the Feast of Tabernacles, which is described as 'the feast of ingathering, at the end of the year' (Exodus 23.16), i.e. the harvest-home. This was the last and greatest feast of the Jewish year and it was sometimes simply referred to as 'the feast'. During this time, the men dwelt in green booths or 'tabernacles' made out of branches, in commemoration of their time in the wilderness when there were no harvests, and they depended daily on God for food.

Today

Harvest Festival is still one of the most popular celebrations, both in town and country. It may seem strange that we bring tinned goods to decorate our place of worship, but these can be a modern way of acknowledging our dependence on God. On the other hand, lumps of coal or sheaves of wheat may evoke memories in older people of harvests of the past, when life was harder and the celebrations more poignant, just as the 'tabernacles' reminded the Israelites of the harder, more dependent times. For all generations a reminder is appropriate of the basic humble elements of soil, water and grain, on which we all depend, and the fruits of which we should share with the poor at this time.

Preparation of Harvest Festival on a farm

For this you need traditional small straw bales. In a barn, put the bales for seating in rows facing an altar table also built up of hay or straw bales, with a white sheet as a cover and a paper frontal decorated by children with a collage or large drawings of animals and tractors. Put items of harvest produce on top. Bales can also be used to make a pulpit, but you need to make sure that they are built up securely! Use an electronic keyboard for the music or invite a local music group if there is one available.

An alternative is to use a cattle shed with a central walkway. The electronic keyboard or music group can be placed on the walkway, and also a choir if you have one. Decorate the barriers with branches. The person taking the service can stand on the walkway, or else use a pickup or trailer which can also be decorated.

Arrange for refreshments to be served at the end – cider, coffee, home-made cakes or biscuits, etc.

Involvement of children

Preparation

If you have a Sunday School or similar group of children, you can ask them to make placards, each bearing a letter of the word HARVEST. It is effective if each background is a different colour or the letters themselves are picked out in different colours. The placards can be plain or elaborate, depending on age, ability and time available.

In addition, ask the children what colours they associate with Harvest and then make some simple banners out of coloured silky material and bean poles. If there aren't enough children to carry banners, adults may be involved.

Prepare a stand where the placards can be put for everyone to see and the banners supported.

At the beginning of the service

The worship Leader and choir are followed by the children with their own leader. They carry the banners and their placards, with the letters hidden. The children face the congregation in a row, with the banner carriers at each end.

Leader	Let's start at the very beginning:
	when the farmer plants his seeds,
	the things that he sows,
	they grows and grows!
	Good things to eat,
	oh what a treat!
Children	**What a treat!**
Leader	What a treat!
	Oh praise the Lord
	who gives us food.
	Praise the Lord!
Children	**Praise the Lord!**

As the children's leader says each letter, a child holds up the appropriate placard and all the children say the words.

Leader	H.
All	**H.**
	H is for . . .
Leader	A.
All	**A.**
	A is for . . .

and so on, until all seven letters are displayed.

All	**H is for Honey and Hands worn by toil.**
	A is for Apples red, green and gold.
	R is for Rhubarb and Raspberries too.
	V is for Veggies all crisp and clean.
	E is for Eggs, from duck, hen and goose.
	S is for Strawberries and Spuds for our chips.
	T is for Turnips feeding people and sheep.
	Spelling HARVEST – thank you God!

The children put their placards on the stand in the same order and the banners are put into their holders.

At the end of the service

The children come forward and take up their letters and banners and go out with their own leader, the worship leader and the choir.

A children's talk

Letters are held up to make the word H A R V E S T.

Leader   What makes a good harvest?

To answer this question, the letters are rearranged to spell H A V E.

List or ask children to name the many things we have from God for which we're grateful, including:

- food and clean water;
- insects to pollinate plants;
- rain to help them grow;
- sun to ripen them.

The letters are then rearranged to spell S T A R V E as we remember:

- the people who don't have the things we have;
- the birds who starve from lack of food when the insects they eat are poisoned.

The letters are then rearranged again to spell S H A R E.

Leader   We share God's earth with other people and with all other creatures.

   What do we have when we share what we have with those who starve?

Letters are held up to make the word H A R V E S T again.

All   **That's what makes a good harvest!**

(Christian Ecology Link Publications)

Harvest Festival Service

Preparation

Arrange for different people to bring specific items as offerings.
The prayers should be said by those bringing up the gifts. The
first items should be earth (soil) and water, without which there
could be no life at all. There are four other offerings: bread and
cereal or grains, wine and oil, fruit and vegetables, eggs and milk.
Other products such as wool, beer or cider could be substituted
for the above.

Welcome and Opening (based on verses from Genesis 1, RSV)

And God said, 'Let the earth put forth vegetation: plants
yielding seed, and fruit trees of every kind on earth that bear
fruit with seed in it.' And it was so. And God said, 'See, I have
given you every plant yielding seed that is upon the face of the
earth, and every tree with seed in its fruit; you shall have them
for food. And to every beast of the earth, every bird of the air,
every creeping thing, everything that has the breath of life, I
have given every green plant for food.' And it was so. God saw
that it was good.

Hymn

'Come, ye thankful people, come' (HO&N 133)

Prayer

Almighty God and Creator,
you only can make the seeds to grow
and the land to bring forth the crops for our sustenance.
On you we rely for the warmth of the sun,
the refreshing life-giving rain,
for our well-being.
Teach us the valuable lesson of humility,
that we may work always and only
in harmony with your law. *We are s any - - - -*
~~Make us righteous and just to all of your creation.~~
We give thanks and praise for your loving kindness

and for the bounty of this harvest.
We bring before you these offerings
in joy and gladness.

The first offering of soil and water is brought up, blessed and laid
on the altar table.

Offering Prayer

Lord, out of the emptiness you brought forth all that we need
for life. Accept these offerings of earth and water as a token of
our gratitude for your loving renewal of them in the face of
our failure to care properly for your creation. **Amen.**

Reading

Humanity, like the rest of organic life, exists on earth for the
needs and purposes of the earth . . . Only thought as
theoretical and as far removed as modern European thought
could have conceived the evolution of [humankind] to be
possible *apart from surrounding nature*, or have regarded the
evolution of humankind as gradual *conquest of nature*. This is
quite impossible. In living, in dying, in evolving, in
degenerating, [humankind] equally serves the purposes of
nature.

(George Ivanovitch Gurdjieff, quoted by James George in *Asking for the
Earth*)

or

The earth is at the same time mother, she is mother of all that
is natural, mother of all that is human. She is the mother of
all, for contained in her are the seeds of all. The earth of
humankind contains all moistness, all verdancy, all
germinating power. It is in so many ways fruitful. All creation
comes from it. Yet it forms the basic raw material for
humankind but also the substance of the incarnation of God's
son.

(Hildegard of Bingen, 1098–1179)

Hymn

'Praise, O praise our God and King' (HO&N 566) *or*
'When God made the garden of creation' (HO&N 910)

The second offering of bread and grains or seeds is brought up, blessed and laid on the altar table.

Offering Prayer

Almighty and ever-loving God, though we may scatter the seeds on the land, though we tend and care for them; still without your aid they would lie barren and dead. We offer this grain and this bread as symbols of remembrance of this truth. Let us never forget that without you, we too are as dried grain on barren land. **Amen.**

Reading

Every thought-seed sown or allowed to fall into the mind, and to take root there, produces its own, blossoming sooner or later into act, and bearing its own fruitage of opportunity and circumstance. Good thoughts bear good fruit and bad thoughts bad fruit. The outer world of circumstances shapes itself to the inner world of thought, and both pleasant and unpleasant external conditions are factors which make for the ultimate good of the individual. As the reaper of [its] own harvest, [humankind] learns both by suffering and bliss. Following the desires, aspirations and thoughts by which one allows oneself to be dominated . . . a person at last arrives at their fruition and fulfilment in the outer condition of life.

(from James Allen, *As a Man Thinketh*)

or

There is no such thing as 'my' bread. All bread is *ours* and is given to me, to others through me, and to me through others. For not only bread, but all things necessary for sustenance in this life, are given on loan to us with others, and because of others and for others, and to others through us.

(Meister Eckhart, 1290–1329)

Hymn

'I am the bread of life' (HO&N 299) *or*
'Bread of Heaven, on thee we feed' (HO&N 82) *or*
'We plough the fields and scatter' (alternative version on page
136)

Offering Prayer

The third offering of wine and oil is brought up, blessed and
placed upon the altar table.

> Lord Jesus, just as this wine and this oil, pressed from fruits
> dispersed upon the boughs, gave you and your followers joy
> and light, so too it is a reminder of all that you gave for us.
> Take us, our bodies and our souls, to be crushed and poured
> out for your glory and service in the world. **Amen.**

Reading (based on verses from Leviticus 25, 26, 31, Numbers 35, Exodus 20, Deuteronomy 5)

> The Lord commands, 'The land shall keep a Sabbath to the
> Lord; every seventh day and every seventh year shall be a
> Sabbath for the Lord; you will neither sow your fields nor
> prune your vineyard. If you obey my laws and keep my
> commandments, then I will reward you with rains in their
> season, and the land shall yield her produce and the trees of
> the field shall yield their fruit. And I will give peace in the
> land. If you remember that the land is sacred and you do not
> pollute nor defile the land on which you dwell, if you allow
> your beasts to rest and respect them and your servants, then
> you will prosper. But if you disobey me and do not allow the
> land to rest and recover, then I will make your cities into
> wastelands, and bring your sanctuaries unto desolation. The
> land will also be in desolation and the people will be scattered
> in desolate places and among strangers and enemies. Then
> the land will lie barren and enjoy her Sabbath rest, because
> you did not allow her to rest whilst you dwelt upon her.'

Hymn

'Now the green blade riseth' (HO&N 475)

The fourth offering of fruit and vegetables is brought up, blessed
and placed with the other offerings.

Offering Prayer

Almighty God, you have provided for us an abundance of
good food. We give thanks for the variety and freshness of all
the things we are able to enjoy in our daily diets, and we offer
these fruits and vegetables as a sign of our appreciation of
your great goodness. May we never forget to care for those
who have little or nothing in this world. **Amen.**

Reading

Remember the poor when you look out on the fields you own,
On your plump cows grazing.
Remember the poor when you look into your barn,
At the abundance of your harvest.
Remember the poor when the wind howls and the rain falls,
As you sit warm and dry in your house.
Remember the poor when you eat fine meat
And drink fine ale at your fine carved table.

The cows have grass to eat;
The rabbits have burrows for shelter;
The birds have warm nests;
But the poor have no food except what you feed them,
No shelter except your house when you welcome them,
No warmth except your glowing fire.

(Author unknown)

Hymn

'I the Lord of sea and sky' (HO&N 332)

The fifth and final offering of milk and eggs is brought up,
blessed and placed upon the altar table.

BLESSING.

Offering Prayer

Great Creator, we give thanks and praise for the beauty of all your creation. All that we offer to you is your own, and yet we know that you, in your great love and mercy, will look kindly upon us and our offerings. Take them and us to be a sign in this your world, symbols of your power and mercy. **Amen**.

Reading

May the Lord bless you

The botany teacher often led his young people through woods and by streams. One morning, when they had been considering the dragonfly, he had told them how, in many years of outdoor study, he had never seen a dragonfly lay eggs. One small boy felt sad for his teacher. And then, soon after, a little miracle happened: a dragonfly alighted on the teacher's hand and then moved on to a near-by leaf and injected her eggs.

Many years later, the pupil remembered that moment of wonder when he heard someone read a story of Celtic times. In that story it was related that St Kevin had gone to a very lonely place to keep Lent. There he lived in a poor hut, where he would kneel to pray, his arm stretched through the window, hand open to heaven.

One day a blackbird settled on Kevin's hand and began to lay. With all gentleness and patience, Kevin cupped his hand, kept his arm steady, and was careful not to disturb her all the days until her young were hatched.

When the story was read, there was, not surprisingly, discussion about elements of exaggeration in tales of the saints. But the man who remembered the dragonfly knew that there are moments when we can enter a world of love and trust between the species, and see miracles. He was struck by the thought that it was as Kevin knelt before God, quiet and open, that the wild creatures had come to him in perfect trust. And as Kevin lived in love for God, so he was filled with love for all God's creatures.

The importance of an animal, and indeed of any creature, is that it is part of God's world, loved by him. If we respect and care for a creature, we are in harmony with God. We receive much blessing. If we despise and abuse an animal, we close ourselves off from the good world. We lose touch with God. We injure all our relationships.

(from John Eaton, *The Circle of Creation*)

Hymn

'Morning has broken' (HO&N 450) *or*
'We are not our own' (HO&N 710)

Blessing

It is suggested that this service be followed by either a harvest supper in a nearby hall, or the serving of bread and cheese, with a selection of cold drinks, in the church or chapel.

Wild harvest

Background

The emphasis at the time of Harvest Festival or Harvest Thanksgiving is normally on food produced for human beings from fields, gardens and greenhouses, but what about God's abundant harvest which will go primarily to wild creatures, although some of it can be stored and eaten by humans? Harvest is a suitable time to say thank you for the foods that will keep wild birds and animals alive during the winter.

Examples are: berries, nuts, mushrooms, hips and haws, sloes, acorns, crab apples, etc., and the wines, jams and jellies that can be made from them.

Preparation

The following is designed for a Sunday School but could be done by a group of adults and children together. It would need to be started some weeks before Harvest Festival, and if not being done by a Sunday School, might make a good activity for the summer holidays.

Go around your locality and identify as many items as possible that can make up your Wild Harvest. Draw up a list and share it with your Sunday School, before making a decision about which ones to pick. Try to get the number to be the same as the children, or else put the children in pairs.

For younger children, produce labels and a large picture which can act as a frontal for a table. The children can then colour these. Older children can make and colour their own labels and do some of the drawing and colouring of the large picture. Include some of the creatures which benefit from the seeds or berries.

Some offerings can be gathered in advance; some will need to be collected on the Friday or Saturday of the Harvest Festival weekend. On the Saturday or before the service, set up a table with the completed frontal and labels. At the beginning of the service, bring up the children and their offerings in pairs and use some of the following prayers. At the end of the service, encourage the congregation to look at the table and talk to the children.

Prayers

1. Each child in turn says one of these prayers. Select those you think most appropriate.

Thank you God for food which grows ready for us to pick and eat.

Thank you God for planning a world where people could just eat the fruit from the trees, without any hard work, before evil came on the scene.*

Thank you God for all the different fruits and tastes, some sweet, some nutty, some strong, some mild, so we are not bored with our food.

---

* If this prayer is used, some preparation of the children as to its significance may be desirable. Alternatively, these children's prayers may be said after the second prayer, which may also help adults to appreciate the meaning.

Thank you God for the trees and bushes which spread out
their arms to offer food to us, without asking whether we
deserve it or not, for they remind us of you.

Thank you God for making us wait for this food, until the
right time.

Thank you God for so much food for free. We could not pick
it all.

Thank you God for giving some food we can eat, but some
only the birds and animals can eat, making us share your gifts
from nature.

Thank you God for the wild birds and animals, which you feed
by these [nuts] [berries] [apples].

2. O God our Creator, we praise you for planning a world where
wild food would feed us, without the need for any hard work,
and where we would talk with you in the cool of the evening.
We worship and praise you that in your love you share
everything, and took the risk that it would all go wrong on you.
We thank you that you cared so much for us and for the world
you have created, that you came yourself as a human being,
Jesus, to suffer the consequences of evil, and to overcome
death, decay and misery.
We glorify you that you raised him from the dead, and that his
resurrected body became the first-fruits of your new creation,
where once again we will eat without having to toil, and we will
talk with you face to face; to you be glory and praise for ever
and ever. **Amen.**

3. We present to you, O Lord, these our offerings of [berries,]
[nuts] [and] [apples]*, together with the [jams,] [puddings]
[and] [cooked food] which we have made from them. They
are our wild harvest, and you are the Lord of the Harvest.
We bless you for all the ways you provide for us, and for this
reminder to us of our dependence on your whole creation.
In the name of the Father, the Son and the Holy Spirit. **Amen.**

---

* Adapt prayer where a star (*) appears.

4. We present to you, O Lord, these our offerings of [berries,]
   [nuts] [and] [apples,] [together with the shells of nuts,]*
   which are eaten by small wild animals who live around us.
   They too have a harvest, and some, like us, will store away
   produce for the winter.
   We thank you for leading us into better understanding of their
   ways and needs, and for your sense of fun in creating them to
   play as well as survive.
   We rejoice in the surroundings you have given us, and offer
   these examples of their wild harvest in our worship of God our
   Creator, Sustainer and Redeemer. **Amen.**

5. We present to you, O Lord, these our offerings of [berries,]
   [nuts] [and] [apples,] [together with the shells of nuts,]*
   which are eaten by the birds who live around us. They have no
   storehouse or barn, and yet you feed them. They get fat with
   the harvest, so they can survive the winter.
   Increase our faith, so that we trust you to provide our daily
   bread if we seek first your kingdom and your righteousness,
   through Jesus Christ our Lord. **Amen.**

6. O God the Creator and Sustainer of the world, who provides
   sufficient food for our need but not for our greed, bless your
   wild creation so that it yields a rich harvest for all your
   dependent creatures, and sufficient for our needs; and give us
   such a feeling of gratefulness that we do not spoil their
   environment nor their harvest.
   Give us generous hearts to recognize the needs of others, and
   open our hands to help, knowing that in others we see the
   eyes of our Lord and Saviour Jesus Christ. **Amen.**

Hymns

We thank thee, Lord, for this fair earth

We thank thee, Lord, for this fair earth,
The glittering sky, the silver sea;
For all their beauty, all their worth,
Their light and glory, come from thee.

Thanks for the flowers that clothe the ground,
The trees that wave their arms above,
The hills that gird our dwellings round,
As thou dost gird thine own with love.

Yet teach us still how far more fair,
More glorious, Father, in thy sight,
Is one pure deed, one holy prayer,
One heart that owns thy Spirit's might.

So, while we gaze with thoughtful eye
On all the gifts thy love has given,
Help us in thee to live and die,
By thee to rise from earth to heaven.

(Author unknown; metre 8888)
Tune: Truro ('Jesus shall reign' – HO&N 359) or 'Awake my soul' (HO&N 58)

We plough the fields and scatter (alternative words)

We plough the fields with tractors,
With drills we sow the land;
But growth is still the wondrous gift
Of God's almighty hand.
We add our fertilizers
To help the growing grain;
But for its full fruition,
It needs God's sun and rain.
All good gifts around us
Are sent from heaven above,
Then thank the Lord, O thank the Lord
For all his love.

With many new machines now
We do the work each day;
We reap the fields with combines,
We bale the new-mown hay.
But still it's God who gives us
Inventive skill and drives
Which lighten labour's drudgery
And give us better lives.
Chorus

He only is the maker
Of galaxies and stars;
Of birds and beasts and flowers,
And any life on Mars.
Atomic powers obey him,
Yet still the birds are fed;
By him our prayer is answered:
Give us our daily bread.
Chorus

We thank thee then, O Father,
For life so rich and good,
For seedtime and the harvest,
The wealth of daily food.
No gifts have we to offer
Such as thy love imparts,
But what thou most desirest:
Our humble, thankful hearts.
Chorus

(Frank Low, 1912–)
Tune: Wir pflügen ('We plough the fields')

Thank you, God, for water, soil and air

Thank you, God, for water, soil and air,
Large gifts supporting everything that lives.
Forgive our spoiling and abuse of them.
Help us renew the face of the earth,
Help us renew the face of the earth.

Thank you, God, for minerals and ores,
The basis of all building, wealth and speed.
Forgive our reckless plundering and waste.
Help us renew the face of the earth,
Help us renew the face of the earth.

Thank you, God, for priceless energy,
Stored in each atom, gathered from the sun.
Forgive our greed and carelessness of power.
Help us renew the face of the earth,
Help us renew the face of the earth.

Thank you, God, for weaving nature's life
Into a seamless robe, a fragile whole.
Forgive our haste, that tampers unawares.
Help us renew the face of the earth,
Help us renew the face of the earth.

Thank you, God, for making planet Earth
A home for us and ages yet unborn.
Help us to share, consider, save and store.
Come and renew the face of the earth.
Come and renew the face of the earth.

(Brian A. Wren, 1936– ; metre 9 10 10 9 9)
Tune: Amstien by John Weaver

Thank you, Father, for your care

Thank you, Father, for your care,
Meeting needs throughout this year.
Make us thankful for our bread,
Grateful lives so richly fed.

Jesus, bless all those who toil
Raising livestock, tilling soil.
Theirs a work from ages past;
While men eat their work must last.

Spirit, pierce our heart to feel
Distant hunger painful, real.
Help us share that they may live
From the blessings that you give.

Warmth and water, soil and seed,
Life and beauty, all we need.
For our future and our food,
Keep our world diverse and good.

Loving God, almighty Lord,
Be by all you made adored;
We who your blessed image bear
Praise you always, everywhere.

(Tony Ingleby; 1948– ; metre 7777)
Tune: Buckland ('Loving Shepherd of thy sheep')

Another harvest hymn

'Now join we, to praise the Creator' (HO&N 471)

St Francis of Assisi

Background

We need to remember that St Francis' love of the whole created order came directly from his love of the Creator. As he walked the countryside in his native Umbria, he was aware of earth and sky, rocks and streams, animals and birds, trees and flowers, and he saw all these as part of the mighty creative work of God and as called to praise God.

He saw animals and birds as sharing in God's gifts and he called them his brothers and sisters. Unlike many of his contemporaries in the thirteenth century, he had very strong feelings about the way animals were treated. His love for his human brothers and sisters was even stronger and his life was dedicated to bringing them to repentance; he considered that one way of showing their love for their Maker should be to treat all God's creatures in a loving manner.

Today

St Francis is seen as the patron saint of birds and animals, and no doubt this is acceptable to him, although he would probably ask us to remember the less appealing creatures: worms and bugs as well as swallows, rats and toads as well as lambs. However, he would be very saddened by the idea that you could look at the created order without reference to the One who made it.

His feast day is 4 October and so while animal services can be held at any time of the year, the autumn seems the right and proper time. Because St Francis' sermon to the birds is so well known, a different reading about him is given, as well as readings about some of the many other saints who also had loving relationships with God's creatures.

Open-air Animal Service

The name Animal Service is probably to be preferred to Pet Service, which limits the scope, especially in rural areas.

Preparation

First of all, decide on the venue – whether indoors or out of doors. Very successful services have been held inside, the only possible snag being the risk of accidents. So long as there are good waterproof floor coverings, this should not present a major problem.

Out-of-door services are subject to the vagaries of our climate and so we need to pray for a fine day, but it should take more than a few drops of rain to dampen the spirits. One open-air service which took place was interrupted when the heavens opened and everybody dashed for cover singing 'Our God reigns'! Any open space will do, but perhaps the best is an uncluttered piece of ground in the churchyard.

There is a lot to be said for having as wide a variety of animals as possible, in the tradition of *The Vicar of Dibley*. Not only dogs and cats but horses, donkeys, cows, goats, sheep, ducks, hens, ferrets, rabbits, hamsters, even insects in bottles can all add to the occasion. It is probably a good idea to have pens for farmyard animals which are not used to being held by hand or staying still. Geese can be pretty vicious, and free-range snakes might be a bit too adventurous, though there is no reason why the latter shouldn't be included if they are well cooped up.

An Animal Service is a wonderful opportunity to give young people a prominent part in an all-age service, and it is good to give pet owners the chance to have their animals blessed with their names, if they have them. It is also good to invite people who do not normally attend services, as the service has a very wide appeal beyond the regular congregation, and people can see the Church becoming relevant to their daily lives.

Welcome

Responses

The earth is the Lord's:
And all that is therein.
He made birds and cattle and all creeping things:
The birds of the air and the fish in the sea.
He made them all and delights in them:
**He made them to be our brothers and sisters
and to glorify him.**

Prayer

For those, O Lord, the humble beasts that bear with us the
burden and heat of the day, and offer their guileless lives for
the well-being of humankind; and for the wild creatures whom
you have made wise, strong and beautiful, we pray for them
your great tenderness of heart, for you have promised to save
both man and beast, and great is your loving kindness,
O Master, Saviour of the World. **Amen.**

(St Basil, Bishop of Caesarea, 330–379)

or

O Lord, we pray now for your blessing and protection upon all
those who work for animal welfare and in animal sanctuaries.
Bless and protect those animals which are exploited for money
or for pleasure, those which help and comfort humanity, and
those engaged in daily work. We remember too animals at risk
in the detection of crime or medical experiments, and those
killed in times of war. **Amen.**

Hymn

'Go tell all creatures in the world' (page 149)

Old Testament Reading: Balaam and his donkey (Numbers 22.20–35, NIV)

This can be performed as a dramatized reading with five voices:
Narrator, God, Angel, Balaam and the Donkey.

That night God came to Balaam and said, 'Since these men have come to summon you, go with them, but do only what I tell you.'

Balaam got up in the morning, saddled his donkey and went with the princes of Moab. But God was very angry when he went, and the angel of the LORD stood in the road to oppose him. Balaam was riding on his donkey, and his two servants were with him. When the donkey saw the angel of the LORD standing in the road with a drawn sword in his hand, she turned off the road into a field. Balaam beat her to get her back on the road.

Then the angel of the LORD stood in a narrow path between two vineyards, with walls on both sides. When the donkey saw the angel of the LORD, she pressed close to the wall, crushing Balaam's foot against it. So he beat her again.

Then the angel of the LORD moved on ahead and stood in a narrow place where there was no room to turn, either to the right or to the left. When the donkey saw the angel of the LORD, she lay down under Balaam, and he was angry and beat her with his staff. Then the LORD opened the donkey's mouth, and she said to Balaam, 'What have I done to you to make you beat me these three times?'

Balaam answered the donkey, 'You have made a fool of me! If I had a sword in my hand, I would kill you right now.'

The donkey said to Balaam, 'Am I not your own donkey, which you have always ridden, to this day? Have I been in the habit of doing this to you?'

'No,' he said.

Then the LORD opened Balaam's eyes, and he saw the angel of the LORD standing in the road with his sword drawn. So he bowed low and fell face down.

The angel of the LORD asked him, 'Why have you beaten your donkey these three times? I have come here to oppose you because your path is a reckless one before me. The donkey saw me and turned away from me these three times. If she had not turned away, I would certainly have killed you by now, but I would have spared her.'

Balaam said to the angel of the LORD, 'I have sinned. I did not realise you were standing in the road to oppose me. Now if you are displeased, I will go back.'

The angel of the LORD said to Balaam, 'Go with the men, but speak only what I tell you.'

or

Animals and humans living together in peace
(Isaiah 11.6–9, NIV)

The wolf will live with the lamb, the leopard will lie down with the goat, the calf and the lion and the yearling together; and a little child will lead them. The cow will feed with the bear, their young will lie down together, and the lion will eat straw like the ox. The infant will play near the hole of the cobra, and the young child put his hand into the viper's nest. They will neither harm nor destroy on all my holy mountain, for the earth will be full of the knowledge of the LORD as the waters cover the sea.

Hymn

'O Lord of every shining constellation' (HO&N 512)

Creation Psalm

Praise the Lord, O my soul!
Oh Christ, my Lord, how great you are!

Women   You looked at the sparrows, of little account in the trading place, and saw how not one is forgotten by God.

Men   You watched the ravens, feeding, neither sowing the seed nor gathering in the harvest, and saw how God provides for them.

Women   You walked in grassy places, delighting in the wild flowers, and saw how God has made them all more beautiful than the finest of fine clothes.

Men   You looked at the fig tree, with its leaves growing green and tender, and you taught of the approach of the kingdom of God.

Women   You discerned in the tiny mustard seed, which grows to become the largest of plants, the hidden growth of the kingdom of God.

Men	You observed flocks of wandering sheep, reminding you of other flocks in need of shepherds.
Women	Your heart was touched by a clucking mother hen fussing over her brood of chicks, and remembered it when you wept for Jerusalem.
Men	You chose a humble donkey as your mount when you entered the city through crowds that acclaimed you.
All	**Praise the Lord, O my soul!** **Oh Christ, my Lord, how great you are!**

Hymn

'All creatures of our God and King' (HO&N 6) (selected verses)

New Testament Reading: The Good Shepherd (based on verses from John 10)

I am the good shepherd. I call my sheep by name and lead them out. The sheep know my voice and follow me. The hired hand is not the shepherd who owns the sheep, so when he sees the wolf coming, he abandons the sheep and runs away. Then the wolf attacks the flock and scatters it. I am the good shepherd; I know my sheep and my sheep know me. I lay down my life for my sheep.

Hymn

'Loving Shepherd of thy sheep' (HO&N 434)

Talk

Rejoicing with our Animals (pages 146–7) *or*
Stories of the Saints (pages 147–9)

Blessing of Animals

Praised be the Creator, who has made every animal
wise in the instinct he has given it.
Now, O God, we pray that you will protect
and bless all things that have breath,
especially these animals gathered here;

guard them from all evil
and grant that they live in peace. **Amen.**

(After Albert Schweitzer)

Hymn

'Jesus shall reign' (HO&N 359)
A collection may be taken for an animal charity.

Blessing

May God bless the sun that is above us,
the earth that is below us,
the creatures all around us,
and lead us all into his peace. **Amen.**

....

Rejoicing with our Animals

We must remember that God created and delighted in animals
long before human beings ever appeared on the earth, and
even today most animals exist, not for the use that the human
race can make of them, but as creations of a living, exuberant
and loving God. In the book of Job (38.39–40.4), God speaks
to Job about his creation and Job is filled with wonder and
praise. And remember, Jesus tells the disciples that God is
aware even of sparrows, insignificant as they may seem
(Matthew 10.29). This is the God who, in the person of Jesus,
came to earth to give us life more abundantly (John 10.10).

You all know the story of the Flood and how Noah went into
the ark with not only his family but also representatives of the
animal kingdom. But do you also know that when the flood
subsided, God made a covenant with Noah which included all
the animal creation? You can read this for yourself in Genesis
9, verses 8 to 17. Can we doubt that the *new* covenant which
Jesus sealed in his blood also covers the whole creation? St
Paul certainly sees Jesus as reconciling God and the whole of
creation (Colossians 1.20) and we are offered the picture of a

new heaven and a new earth in the book of Revelation (21.1ff., also 2 Peter 3.13). What kind of a new creation would it be if there were no animals or birds or plants or stars?

You have come today because, like Job, you are filled with wonder and praise for the animals which God has created, but more than that, because you also rejoice in the companionship they provide and the way in which God allows them to be of use to human beings.

You are also acting out the words of Isaiah when he prophesied that one day people and nature would live in harmony: 'And the wolf shall dwell with the lamb and the leopard shall lie down with the kid . . . and a little child shall lead them.' You can find the whole passage in the book of Isaiah, chapter 11, verses 1 to 9 [leave out this sentence if the passage from Isaiah has been read]. So perhaps, when you go home today, you can think that not only have you praised God for the particular animals which he has entrusted to your care but you've also taken part in a service in which we have a glimpse of heaven. This is how God intended his creation to be, and indeed how it will be when the long days of frustration spoken of by St Paul are over and all things are made new (Romans 8.18–23).

Stories of the Saints

Melangell* and the Hare

This requires two voices: Narrator and Prince.

In 604, the Prince of Powys went hunting at Pennant. His hounds chased a hare into the thicket of thorns where Melangell had built her hermit's hut. He discovered Melangell sheltering the hare under the folds of her cloak as she prayed. The Prince shouted to his hounds, 'Catch the hare, catch the hare,' but they must have sensed a presence more powerful than their instinct, for they gradually went further and further away.

---

* Pronounced 'Mel*an*geth' in Welsh ('th' as in 'think').

The Prince was astonished. He asked the young woman, 'Who are you?', and Melangell told him her story. This made a deep impression on him and he said, 'Because Almighty God was pleased to protect this little hare through you, I will give you land to use for the service of God and also as a sanctuary for animals.'

(Based on the story of Melangell in E. R. Henken, *Traditions of Welsh Saints*)

(In time the hermit's hut was replaced by a church which you can visit at Pennant Melangell in Powys.)

St Mungo and the Robin

As Mungo grew up, he learned some invaluable lessons from his mother Tannoc. Long walks with her by the river and the forests were his college. He learned the names of flowers and their seasons, the feeding and mating habits of birds and beasts and how to win the confidence of the furred and feathered creatures. Mungo learnt to understand animals, fish and birds from his heart and used this gift throughout his life.

It was first seen when he was a boy in Culross. One day some robins were pecking at the ground for scraps, and some village boys were throwing stones at them. One bird was hit and fell to the ground. The boys ran away but Mungo picked up the fallen bird, caressed its feathers and prayed, 'Lord Jesus Christ, in whose hands is the breath of every creature, tame or wild, give back to this bird the breath of life, that your name may be glorified.' After a little while, the bird revived and flew away.

(Based on R. B. Hale, *The Beloved St Mungo*)

St Francis and the Wolf of Gubbio

This requires two voices: Narrator and St Francis.

The land around the town of Gubbio was plagued by a large and hungry wolf which attacked not only animals but people, until they hardly dared to venture beyond the walls.

St Francis came to the town and, hearing about the wolf, went out to meet it. The wolf came running with its mouth open, but when St Francis made the sign of the cross, the power of

God checked the wolf, so that it closed its terrible jaws and lay down at the saint's feet. St Francis said to it: 'Brother Wolf, you have done great harm, so that the whole town is your enemy, but I want to make peace between you and them; if you give a pledge not to harm them any more, I will ask the people to promise to feed you every day.' The wolf showed, by moving its body, tail and ears, that it willingly accepted what the saint had said. Then St Francis said: 'Brother Wolf, I order you, in the name of the Lord Jesus, to come with me now, without fear, into the town.' And the wolf immediately began to walk with the saint, like a very gentle lamb.

St Francis told the townspeople that the wolf had promised to make peace and never hurt them again, if they would feed him. They all promised in a loud voice to feed the wolf every day. From that time forward, the wolf and the people kept the pact. The wolf lived for two years more and it went from door to door for food. When it grew old and died, the people were sorry because its peaceful kindness and patience reminded them of St Francis.

(Based on *The Little Flowers of St Francis*)

Hymn

Go tell all creatures in the world

Go tell all creatures in the world
In ways they understand;
Deal gently with the beasts and birds
Who share the Saviour's land.

That was the message Jesus gave
And he is Lord and King;
Let's tell it by the deeds we do,
The good news that I bring.

Protect his forests, heal the air,
Care for the shining sea,
Arrest our cruelty and our greed
And set its victims free.

So shall our lives proclaim the one
Who sent a little child
To lead all things safe home, in him
Redeemed and reconciled.

To where upon his holy hill
None hurt and none destroy,
And all creation's present groans
Are turned to songs of joy.

(Armorel K. Walling, 1940– ; metre 86 86)
Tune: St Fulbert ('Ye choirs of new Jerusalem' – HO&N 754)

....

Prayers

Suitable prayers will also be found in Carmen Bernos de Gasztold,
Prayers from the Ark.

All Souls

Background

Festivals at this time of year pre-date Christianity in these islands.
For the pagan Celts, the New Year began on 1 November which
was seen as the beginning of winter, and on 31 October – their
'New Year's Eve' – beasts that would not survive the winter were
slaughtered and great bonfires were lit. Burning straw was also
carried around the fields to fertilize them for the following year.
The tradition of lighting bonfires on 31 October was carried on
until the time of the Gunpowder Plot in the seventeenth century
when it moved to Guy Fawkes Night on 5 November.

For Christians there have always been days to remember all the
saints, both known and unknown: on All Saints Day, 1 November,
and then all those who have gone before them, on All Souls,
2 November. In medieval times, when the eve of a festival was
important, the day before All Saints (31 October) was known as
All Hallows Eve, which survives today as Hallowe'en,
unfortunately rarely celebrated in a Christian way. A service held
on Hallowe'en is a good way of reclaiming it.

Preparation

Nightlights are needed for the Commendation (these are
probably easier to manage than small candles). If possible, ask
those who are coming to bring the names of loved ones with
them, printed on a piece of paper; also station someone at the
door with paper and pens for those who have not done so. When
the time comes for the Commendation, this person or another
should stand by the table or prepared floor space with a taper,
and help light the individual nightlights.

All Souls songs of praise

Welcome

Hymn

'The Lord's my shepherd' (HO&N 654)

Reading (verses from 1 Corinthians 15, NRSV)

Now I should remind you, brothers and sisters, of the good news that I proclaimed to you. For I handed on to you as of first importance what I in turn received: that Christ died for our sins in accordance with the scriptures, and that he was buried, and that he was raised on the third day. Christ has been raised from the dead, the first fruits of those who have died. But someone will ask, 'How are the dead raised? With what kind of body do they come?' What you sow does not come to life unless it dies. And as for what you sow, you do not sow the body that is to be, but a bare seed, perhaps of wheat or of some other grain. But God gives it a body as he has chosen and to each kind of seed its own body. Listen, I will tell you a mystery! We will not all die, but we will all be changed, in a moment, in the twinkling of an eye. For the trumpet will sound and the dead will be raised imperishable, and we will be changed. Then the saying that is written will be fulfilled: 'Death has been swallowed up in victory.' 'Where, O death, is your victory? Where, O death, is your sting?' Thanks be to God, who gives us the victory through our Lord Jesus Christ.

or (Revelation 22.1–5, NRSV)

Then the angel showed me the river of the water of life, bright as crystal, flowing from the throne of God and of the Lamb through the middle of the street of the city. On either side of the river is the tree of life with its twelve kinds of fruit, producing its fruit each month; and the leaves of the tree are for the healing of the nations. Nothing accursed will be found there any more. But the throne of God and of the Lamb will be in it, and his servants will worship him; they will see his face, and his name will be on their foreheads. And there will be no more night; they need no light of lamp or sun, for the Lord God will be their light, and they will reign for ever and ever.

Hymn

'O Love that will not let me go' (HO&N 517)

Reading

Judy and her husband were devastated by the death of their son. She says she could never have imagined the intensity of the pain. Twelve months on, the pain had not eased one little bit. From an early age, Michael had struggled with a chemical imbalance, which in his teens led to mental illness. This became so acute that eventually Michael took his own life.

A particular concern for the family was that Michael should be not only happy in the afterlife but whole in every sense. A series of extraordinary events took place at this point. Firstly Michael's doctor, who had treated him for years, began to have vivid dreams about him. Steve, Michael's younger brother, also began to have dreams in which many of the questions they had been asking themselves appeared to be answered. Judy had prayed long and hard for her son to be at peace, and indications in these dreams seemed to point to this being the case. One incredible event then took place that left Judy and her family in no doubt whatsoever that Michael was at peace and happy.

It was very early on a bright summer morning that Steve awoke. He drifted up from sleep slowly and sat up in bed. Rubbing his eyes, he watched in disbelief as his bedroom door slowly opened. This happened in a controlled manner and completely unaided. Michael's room was across the hall, and the door of that room was also opened wide. Sitting on the bed was Michael. This was certainly no dream. Steve had had enough dreams of Michael recently to know the difference immediately. Perhaps those dreams had all been to prepare him for this experience.

Michael was dressed all in white and was glowing. Steve describes him as looking as if he was lit from inside by a lamp. His face was pale and smooth, and his features were not as clearly defined as Steve remembered. Staring with fascination and deep intensity so as not to miss any details, Steve was transfixed.

When Steve had come to terms with the sight of his brother, Michael spoke. Softly he said, 'I am here to answer your questions and clarify your dreams.' He went on, 'You may ask anything you wish from me.' Steve remained calm, though excited, and asked many questions. The answers elated and astonished him. Michael tried to explain how different earth and heaven were. Describing the vastness of heaven he said, 'By comparison, you could fit the earth on a pinhead.' Music had always been a close bond between the brothers. Both had played the guitar together for hours. Michael told his brother that music was now so fantastic in the other world that he could never begin to describe it. 'You would never hear anything remotely like it on earth,' he added.

It was then that Steve asked the question everyone wanted an answer to. Was Michael well and at peace? The reply was emphatic: he was in a perfect state of mind, all illness gone. The peace was wonderful and a complete release. With this question answered, Michael was gone and Steve was left so elated that he could scarcely contain his joy.

Leaping out of bed, he rushed into Judy's room, trying to tell her everything at once and no doubt not making much sense at first. Pulling his mother from the bedroom, he led her down the hall to Michael's room and to the exact spot where his brother had been. He had spoken to Steve with such calmness and clarity that they could only marvel and rejoice, remembering the dreadful state he had been in. Judy was elated as Steve struggled to communicate how happy his brother was. Finally he said, 'He is happy beyond anything we can feel on earth.' He had come to the conclusion that Michael had become a higher being, perhaps even an angel. His weak, sick brother was no more, having become strong, intelligent and free from all suffering. Steve could not emphasise enough that he was wide awake during this wonderful time, and there was absolutely no possibility that he had been dreaming.

Even though Michael had gone from the room, Steve and his mother could still feel his presence. All sense of guilt had gone. They now knew for certain that Michael loved them, and that he had, as Judy put it, given them 'soul growth'.

(from Glennyce S. Eckersley, *Children and Angels*)

Hymn

'Ye holy angels bright' (HO&N 755)

Prayer: Open the Gate of Glory

Lord,
When our steps are weary
And the going is rough;
When our life is dreary
And our journey is tough;
Open the gate of glory.

Lord,
When the dark clouds thicken
And the storm rides high;
When the troubles quicken
And danger is nigh;
Open the gate of glory.

Lord,
When our work is completed
And the battle is done;
We are not defeated,
The victory you have won;
Open the gate of glory.

(David Adam, 1936–)

Hymn

'In heavenly love abiding' (HO&N 323)

Prayers

O Lord God, your way is perfect; help us, we pray, always to
trust in your goodness, that walking with you in faith and
following you in all simplicity, we may possess quiet and
contented minds, leaving all our worries with you because you
care for us; for the sake of Jesus Christ our Lord. **Amen.**

Divine Creator, in your son Jesus Christ you have given us a
true faith and a sure hope. Strengthen this faith and hope in
us all our days, that we may live as those who believe in the
communion of saints, the forgiveness of sins and the
resurrection to eternal life, through your son Jesus Christ our
Lord. **Amen.**

Commendation (based on Romans 8.38–9)

There is nothing in death or life,
in the world as it is or the world as it shall be,
nothing in all creation that can separate us
from the love of God in Jesus Christ our Lord.

In that confidence, therefore, we commend our loved ones:

At this point, the names of all the loved ones who are to be
remembered at this service are read out. If a relative or a friend is
present, they are invited to come and light a nightlight. If not, the
minister or a helper lights the nightlight. This may be done for
each person remembered, or, if there are too many names, each
person lights just one light for all their friends and relations.

Let us all join in the Lord's Prayer.

The Lord's Prayer (page 227)

Hymn

'Thine be the glory' (HO&N 672)

Prayer

May Christ support us all the day long
until the shadows lengthen,
and the evening comes,
and the busy world is hushed,
the fever of life is over
and our work is done.
Then in his mercy,
may he grant us safe lodging,
a holy rest
and peace at the last,
through Jesus Christ our Lord. **Amen.**

Blessing

Our Lord Jesus Christ be with you to defend you,
within you to keep you,
before you to lead you,
beside you to guard you.
May he be your comfort and strength,
your hope and support,
your light and your way,
in the days that lie ahead.
And may the blessing of God Almighty,
Father, Son and Holy Spirit, be upon you
and remain with you,
this day and evermore. **Amen.**

Hymn

'Guide me, O thou great redeemer' (HO&N 252)

COMMUNITY
OCCASIONS

Bell Ringers' Service

Background

The ringing of bells full circle by means of rope and wheel is unique to the British Isles, a few former British colonies and the area around Verona in Italy. Change-ringing in the English-speaking countries has evolved over the last 350 years but some of the changes now rung would be familiar to our predecessors from the seventeenth and eighteenth centuries.

Until the late nineteenth century, most ringing was organized by bands belonging to individual churches or, in major cities of the time such as London, Oxford and Norwich, by bands belonging to groups of churches. Over the last 150 years many societies, based largely on diocesan boundaries, have been established. Most of them are affiliated to the Central Council of Church Bell Ringers which is now an international body. The Council looks after matters of common interest and presents ringing to the general public.

Today

There are over 5,000 rings of five or more bells on which change-ringing can be practised. These are mainly in Anglican churches but there is a growing number of ringers in other Christian traditions, notably the Roman Catholic tradition which has its own bell-ringers' guild. There are about 35,000 active ringers, and probably at least as many who no longer ring. They can keep up to date with ringing news through *The Ringing World*, a journal which has been published weekly since 1911 and is now owned by the Central Council.

A service celebrating bell ringing is suitable for both town and country.

Once the ringers have finished ringing before the service, it is
recommended that they come in with the worship leader
and sit at the front in seats reserved for them.

Song

'Come on and celebrate!' (HO&N 125)

Responses (based on Psalm 98)

Shout for joy to the Lord, all the earth,
burst into jubilant song with music;
make music to the Lord with the harp,
with the harp and sound of bells.
With trumpets and the blast of the ram's horn,
shout for joy before the Lord, the King.
Let the rivers clap their hands,
let the mountains sing together for joy.
Let us all make a joyful noise unto the Lord.

Reading (Colossians 3.12–17, NIV)

Therefore, as God's chosen people, holy and dearly loved,
clothe yourselves with compassion, kindness, humility,
gentleness and patience. Bear with each other and forgive
whatever grievances you may have against one another.
Forgive as the Lord forgave you. And over all these virtues put
on love, which binds them all together in perfect unity. Let the
peace of Christ rule in your hearts, since as members of one
body you were called to peace. And be thankful. Let the word
of Christ dwell in you richly as you teach and admonish one
another with all wisdom, and as you sing psalms, hymns and
spiritual songs with gratitude in your hearts to God. And
whatever you do, whether in word or deed, do it all in the
name of the Lord Jesus, giving thanks to God the Father
through him.

Hymn: Ringing through the year

Give praise to Him, our God on high,
Ring out, let notes on breezes fly.
By our labours through the year
We seek to draw His faithful near.

Our harvest's golden gifts now blest,
Hail Autumn's languid span of rest,
November comes with sombre sounds
And echoes, muffled all around.

On Christmas Eve in midnight air
O'er frosty grass and branches bare,
Sing out the songs of joyous praise
And heavenward hearts of all men raise.

In morning light of early spring
In praise of Jesus Christ our King,
Let these tuneful voices swell
With homage from each herald bell.

When Lent is o'er, with Easter mirth
We celebrate our world's rebirth.
Then Whitsuntide's ascending sound
Through streams of warming air abound.

As Summer's halcyon days roll on,
We honour God in sound and song;
Come morning mists and evening dew
Our lives we dedicate anew.

(Jean Curd, 1940–)
Tune: Gotts Will Machen ('God, whose farm is all creation' – HO&N 236)

A Talk may be given or an excerpt from Chapter 3 of *Akenfield*
by Ronald Blythe may be read.

Prayer

> We praise you Lord, for we are fearfully and wonderfully made.
> As we ring the peal, we co-ordinate our bodies and minds,
> keeping time and controlling the bells,

and our concentration takes away our anxieties and worries.
Lost in your mathematical wonders
and the harmony of our bodies,
we glorify you with enormous noise,
you who did not despise the human body
but glorified it with your own divine presence,
and now reigns, one God, world without end. **Amen.**

Dedication or Re-dedication of the Bells

In the faith of Christ,
and for the benefit of his holy Church,
we (re-)dedicate our bells to the glory of God,
that they may spread the message
of our Creator's joy in new creation,
our Redeemer's restoration of the lost and damaged,
and our Sustainer's help and guidance on our way.
In the name of the Father, and of the Son,
and of the Holy Spirit. **Amen.**

Dedication Prayer of the Bell Ringers

**As bell ringers, we dedicate our energy
and skill to God's glory,
and determine that our ringing work
will be our prayer.
That is our resolve. Amen.**

Let us join together and say the Lord's Prayer.

The Lord's Prayer (page 227)

Dedication Prayer of the People

**As a congregation, we dedicate ourselves
to the glory of God,
our lives ringing out in praise
and calling all people to worship
the One who rejoices in heaven
at the joy of all believers. Amen.**

Hymn

'Thine be the glory' (HO&N 672) *or*
'Angel voices ever singing' (HO&N 37)

Blessing

The bell ringers should go out with the worship leader and ring
again. Those present should be encouraged to stay and listen to
the bells and should be offered refreshments if possible.

Circle Dancing

'Again you will provide yourself with tambourines and go forth with the merry throng of dancers.' (Jeremiah 31.4, REB)

Background

Circle Dancing has been defined as something which may feel different every time you dance. Circle Dancing is dancing together in a circle and is done by folk dancers from many lands. The dances themselves originated with the members of the villages in which they were danced for hundreds of years. Many dances were passed from generation to generation by 'word of foot'. The dances have become part of the culture and living tradition of the people.

With the advent of foreign travel, dance teachers visited these countries and witnessed the dances and brought them away to be shared in circles. Other dances are newly choreographed to both ancient and modern music which moves and inspires the choreographer.

Today

In the middle of the dancing circle, there is usually a 'Centre', where spiritual objects or artefacts are placed. This helps people to keep the shape of the circle and adds to the dancing atmosphere.

The idea of dancing yourself to health and happiness is not new; it is humanity's most ancient method of expressing emotion, releasing tension and celebrating rituals and joyous occasions. Few adults in the West dance spontaneously, for we feel inhibited and are too often afraid of making mistakes. Circle Dancing, however, is not competitive and should not feel threatening. It is about participation, not performance, and leads naturally into religious worship.

Circle Dancing should be introduced gradually, with time to practise, and adapted according to available space and people's mobility. It is suitable for all ages. Most dances will fit in with normal hymns or Celtic music and can become more intricate according to people's ability. The mere holding of hands during the dance should enrich the spiritual experience and improve social bonding among the worshippers.

The two examples given are simple Circle Dances which could be danced to most available music. Celtic or traditional religious music could be used and adapted according to the season. Circle Dancing should ensure that peace and joy emanate from the worship to the rest of humanity.

1. Alouette

Two steps left, one step right; (*repeat*)
Two steps left, two steps right.

2. The Vine

Right foot in, then left foot in;
pass right foot over left foot
and right foot behind left foot;
step left and repeat.

(Tune: Star of County Down)

Moorland Evening Worship

A large part of the United Kingdom consists of moorland, although much of this is uninhabited. However, there are many small communities and places of worship for which this service may be suitable. It was written by The St Michael's (Princetown) Trust on Dartmoor, where it is in regular use. A few words, such as 'tor', may have to be altered to fit moorland in a different part of the country.

....

Welcome

Opening Responses

The sun rises, the mist scatters from the tors:
Praise the God of creation.
The skylark stretches its wings and sings high above the moors:
Praise the God of creation.
The people waken and hasten to the tasks of the day:
Praise the God of creation.
The heather opens and the moor is hazed in purple.
Praise the God of creation.
The clouds dim the light of day and rain caresses the hills:
Praise the God of creation.
The sheep make tracks in the heather and cattle graze the moor:
Praise the God of creation.
The sky darkens, moon and stars share their light:
Praise the God of creation.
The night embraces the land, people rest whilst the fox cries in the night:
Praise the God of creation.

Reading (verses adapted from Psalm 104)

Praise the Lord, O my soul, O Lord my God, you are very great;

**He set the earth on its foundations and clothed it with the
waters.**

He established the uplands and the valleys.

**He makes grass grow for the cattle and plants for man to
cultivate – bringing forth food from the earth:**

wine that gladdens the heart of man, oil to make his face
shine,

and bread that sustains his heart.

**The trees of the Lord are well watered, the rowan of the moor
he tends.**

There the birds make their nests; the heron has its home in
the pine trees.

**The high tors belong to the ring ouzel; the crags are a refuge
for the ponies.**

The moon marks off the seasons and the sun knows when to
go down.

**You bring darkness, it becomes night and the owls glide over
the moor.**

The foxes hunt for their prey and seek their food from God.

**The sun rises and they steal away; they return and lie down in
their dens.**

Then people go out to their work, to their labour until
evening.

**How many are your works, O Lord! In wisdom you made
them all;**

the earth is full of your creatures.

These all look to you to give them their food at the proper
time.

When you give it to them, they gather it up;

when you open your hand, they are satisfied with good things.

When you hide your face, they are terrified;

when you take away their breath, they die and return to the
dust.

When you send your Spirit, they are created,

and you renew the face of the earth.

May the glory of the Lord endure for ever;

may the Lord rejoice in his works –

I will sing to the Lord all my life;

I will sing praise to my God as long as I live.

Confession

We have not cherished the earth,
we have ignored its intricate wonder,
dimmed its splendour and marred its beauty
and given no thought to tomorrow:
Father God, have mercy on your children.

We have become obsessed with what we own
and possessed by what we still covet;
we waste earth's precious resources whilst many want,
and in our failure to act, gamble its future well-being:
Jesus, Son of God, save us from ourselves.

We have lived as if every other living thing
only has breath for our benefit;
we pollute the teeming waters,
cut down the living forest
and condemn your creatures to extinction:
Holy Spirit of God, teach us to live in peace.

As the warm bright rays of the sun
scatter the mist from the hills and tors,
dispel the darkness from our lives,
that we may live as children of light.
In the name of Christ. Amen.

Reading

Supply your own reading and follow it with silent reflection and
prayer.

Silent Reflection and Prayer

Prayer for God's help

The mist enfolds the hills in its mantle:
Embrace us in your love, O Lord.
The rain washes the rocks and leaves:
Cleanse us in your love, O Lord.
The stream flows down to the valley:
Direct us in your love, O Lord.
The granite tor stands firm:

Establish us in your love, O Lord.
The rowan tree clings to the hillside:
Root us in your love, O Lord.
The night veils the moor in darkness:
Hide us in your love, O Lord.
This night and every night:
Hide us in your love, O Lord. Amen.

Closing Responses

The sun has set over the hills of the western sky:
Keep us in your gaze, O Lord.
The evening's shadow falls across the moor:
Keep us in your light, O Lord.
The sky darkens and stars fill the night:
Keep us in your heart, O Lord.
The tracks and paths are left behind:
Keep us in your way, O Lord.
Gracious God, Father, Son and Holy Spirit,
keep us and all your creatures
in your love this night. **Amen.**

Blessing

New Rural Venture

Background

During the past decade or so, the idea of diversification has become increasingly prominent and, in some rural areas, the setting up of new businesses has been a lifeline for struggling families and communities. As well as prayers for new ventures, a prayer is included for a farmer or farming family starting out again after a disaster.

Preparation

Either incorporate the material into an existing service or arrange to visit the site of the new enterprise. The psalms, readings and some of the prayers are also suitable for a town-based enterprise.

Invite friends and neighbours to support those who are 'launching out into the deep' and, if possible, round off the occasion with refreshments, including a toast to the new venture!

....

Psalm (verses from Psalm 40, NIV)

I waited patiently for the Lord;
he turned to me and heard my cry.
He lifted me out of the slimy pit,
out of the mud and the mire.
He set my feet on a rock
and gave me a firm place to stand.
He put a new song in my mouth,
a hymn of praise to our God.
May all those who seek you
rejoice and be glad in you;
may those who love your salvation
always say, 'Great is the Lord'.

or (based on verses from Psalms 100 and 103)

> Shout for joy, all the earth,
> come before the Lord with joyful songs.
> **Give thanks to him, bless his name,**
> **for his steadfast love endures for ever.**
> It is he who made us and we belong to him,
> we are his people and the sheep of his field.
> **Give thanks to him, bless his name,**
> **for his steadfast love endures for ever.**
> He will satisfy our desires with good things
> so that our strength and vigour are renewed.
> **Give thanks to him, bless his name,**
> **for his steadfast love endures for ever.**

New Testament Reading (Luke 5.3b–7, 10b, RSV)

> And Jesus sat down and taught the people from the boat. And
> when he had ceased speaking, he said to Simon, 'Put out into
> the deep and let down your nets for a catch.' And Simon
> answered, 'Master, we toiled all night and took nothing. But at
> your word I will let down the nets.' And when they had done
> this, they enclosed a great shoal of fish; and as their nets were
> breaking they beckoned to their partners in the other boat to
> come and help them. And they came and filled both boats, so
> that they began to sink. And Jesus said to Simon, 'Do not be
> afraid; henceforth you will be catching men.'

Prayers

You may use some or all sections of these prayers.

> O God of new beginnings,
> who brought Joseph out of slavery and prison
> that he might save many from starvation:
> **support us in this new endeavour.**
> O God of new beginnings
> who changed Ruth from a despised alien
> into a founder of the line of David:
> **support us in this new endeavour.**

O God of new beginnings,
who took David from following the sheep
to be the shepherd of your people Israel:
support us in this new endeavour.
O God of new beginnings,
who raised Esther from lowliness to queenship
that she might be the saviour of your people:
support us in this new endeavour.
O God of new beginnings,
who called Peter and Andrew, James and John
to leave their nets and become fishers of men:
support us in this new endeavour.
O God of new beginnings,
who gave Martha, Mary and Lazarus
new roles as Jesus's beloved supporters:*
support us in this new endeavour.
O God of new beginnings,
who took the broken Peter
to be the shepherd of your early church:
support us in this new endeavour. Amen.

or (change words in italics to she/her, he/his, etc.)

O God of new beginnings,
you who always call your children
to move forward in the journey through life;
support [*names*] at this time
as *they* launch out into the deep;
give *them* the same faith and trust
as those who responded to your call in Galilee,
that *they* may find joy and fulfilment
in *their* new enterprise. **Amen.**

---

* See John 11.5. Jesus loved Martha and her sister and Lazarus, and spent his last nights on earth at their house.

Other Prayers

Lord Jesus Christ,
we pray for your blessing
upon this [shop/workshop/restaurant etc.],
that all those who work here,
rejoicing in an atmosphere of hope,
may expend their skill and energy to the utmost,
and that the enterprise itself
may bring blessings to our whole community. **Amen.**

or (to be said by person setting up new enterprise on the land)

**O Creator God, the land and all its creatures
were made by you and are loved by you:
we have been given the privilege
of living in closeness with the earth;
we feel called to set up this new enterprise
of [organic farming/saving rare breeds/a farm shop/
a pick-it-yourself/a nature trail etc.]
and *we* ask for your blessing on it;
so that having before us the vision
of living in harmony with our land [and our animals],
we may work towards bringing your kingdom upon earth.
In the name of Jesus Christ, our Lord. Amen.**

Prayer for a farmer or a farming family starting out again

(replace words in *italics* where required)

O God, whose Son passed through agony and death
to resurrection and the promise of new life;
so we have come through a time of anguish
to a time of renewal and revival.
Look favourably, we pray you, upon [*names*]
as *they* set out once more in hope
to farm *their* land [and tend *their* animals].
Give *them* courage and confidence,
Support *them* with your Holy Spirit,
that *they* may praise you in *their* life and work,
and when that work is done,

they may come at last to your heavenly kingdom.
We ask this in the name of our Lord and Saviour, Jesus Christ.
Amen.

Blessing

Our Lord Jesus Christ be with you to defend you,
within you to keep you,
before you to lead you,
beside you to guard you.
May he be your comfort and strength,
your hope and support,
your light and your way,
in the days that lie ahead.
And may the blessing of God Almighty
be upon you and remain with you
this day and evermore. **Amen.**

or

May God bless your work;
may it help to bring his kingdom
of peace and love here in this place;
and the blessing of God Almighty
rest on you and those working with you,
at this time and in the years to come. **Amen.**

Hymns

'The journey of life may be easy, may be hard', verses 1 and 2
    (JP 468 or CP 45)
'One more step along the world I go' (HO&N 525)
'Father, hear the prayer we offer' (HO&N 161)
'Fight the good fight' (HO&N 169)
'He who would valiant be' (HO&N 281)
'Lead us, heavenly Father, lead us' (HO&N 379)
'Through the night of doubt and sorrow' (HO&N 687)

Parish Councils of England

Background

Unlike their counterparts in some European countries, parish councils have traditionally had limited powers and even more limited resources. However, they are increasingly recognized as a vital part of government with the prospect of a substantially increased role for those councils which can demonstrate their ability to achieve certain 'quality' standards.

The major contribution of parish councils has been to lobby district and county councils to ensure proper delivery of services and to help shape the future development of their communities. However, changing government policy envisages the parish council playing a leading part in the provision of local transport, affordable housing, enhanced recreational facilities and greater access to information technology.

Parish councils which choose to take on these challenges will begin to take on responsibility not only for the provision of many local services but, more fundamentally, for developing strategies to protect and enhance the economic and social well-being of their communities.

A sample of their existing and new spheres of activity could include:

- managing community transport schemes;
- assuming minor areas of highway maintenance;
- supporting child care provision and services for the elderly;
- managing footpath networks;
- providing recycling facilities;
- determining the need for low-cost housing schemes;
- developing sporting and recreational facilities;
- encouraging the development of tourism and economic diversification;
- improving access to information technology;
- developing strategies for the future in the form of Village Appraisals and Plans.

Service for a new parish council

Members of the Council should wait at the back with the minister, and the choir if there is one, then follow the minister to the front where seats are reserved.

Opening Hymn

'Judge eternal, throned in splendour' (HO&N 372)

Welcome

> We come here today to give thanks for the place where we live, and for those people who are prepared to spend their time and energy in the service of us all.

Thanksgiving

> Let us first give thanks for our local community and environment:
> for the beauty of fields, trees and lanes,
> for streams and springs and rivers.
> **We give thanks, O God.**
> For the farms tended through the centuries,
> for the houses where many generations have lived.
> **We give thanks, O God.**
> For new houses bringing new neighbours,
> who can enrich our local life.
> **We give thanks, O God.**
> For village hall and public house*,
> where we can meet together in recreation.
> **We give thanks, O God.**
> For the school(s) where our children are taught
> and the dedication of the teachers and their helpers.
> **We give thanks, O God.**
> For shops and other enterprises,
> which serve the community and provide work.
> **We give thanks, O God.**

---

* If preferred, substitute 'For village hall and other public places' or other appropriate recreational facilities.

Confession

Now let us acknowledge that because we are human, we often fail and need to ask forgiveness.

We have not cared enough for each other:
Lord, have mercy.
We have not cared enough for our local community:
Christ, have mercy.
We have not cared enough for your world:
Lord, have mercy.

Forgiveness of Sins

May God forgive and heal us,
may Jesus be beside us as we walk through life,
and may the Holy Spirit speak to our hearts
and understanding. **Amen.**

Psalm (based on Psalm 72)

Give the king your judgements, O God,
and your righteousness to the king's son.
Then shall he judge your people righteously
and your poor with justice.
May the mountains bring forth peace,
and the little hills righteousness for the people.
May he defend the poor among the people,
deliver the children of the needy and crush the oppressor.
May he come down like rain upon the mown grass,
like the showers that water the earth.
In his time shall righteousness flourish,
and abundance of peace till the moon shall be no more.
He shall have pity on the weak and poor;
he shall preserve the lives of the needy.
He shall redeem their lives from oppression and violence,
and dear shall their blood be in his sight.
Let corn abound throughout the land,
standing thick upon the hilltops;
May its fruit flourish like Lebanon,
and may its grain grow like the grass of the field.

Blessed be the Lord, the God of Israel,
who alone does wonderful things.
And blessed be his glorious name for ever.
May all the earth be filled with his glory.

Reading (from 1 Peter, authors' version)

This is read by the Leader of the Council.

Live in harmony with one another,
be sympathetic, love as brothers and sisters,
have a tender heart and a humble mind.
Show proper respect for everyone.
Fear God and honour the government.
Stand fast in the faith;
Cast all your cares upon God for he cares for you.
And may peace be upon all who are in Christ.

This is the word of the Lord:
Thanks be to God.

Prayers

Let us now ask God to bless those who hold office and power
in our nation:
the Queen and the members of the Royal Household,
the Prime Minister and all other ministers of the Crown,
the members of both Houses of Parliament.
Lord, in your mercy:
Hear our prayer.
Let us pray for civil servants and local government officers
who plan for the future of our towns and villages,
those elected to local government in county and district,
those who serve on Parish Councils as our representatives.
Lord, in your mercy:
Hear our prayer.
Let us pray for teachers and those involved in our school(s),
governors and staff,
all who work for the benefit of our children.
Lord, in your mercy:
Hear our prayer.

Let us pray for ministers and all who serve in places of worship,
those running clubs and societies,
all who work to make our village safer and more beautiful.
Lord, in your mercy:
Hear our prayer.

An Address or Reading may follow (see end of service).

Hymn and Offertory

'For the healing of the nations' (HO&N 186)

Offertory to be given to a local charity or cause chosen by the Council.

Prayers

Members of the Parish Council stand.

O God, the Creator of all people and the Ruler of all things, we
present to you the members of the Parish Council who have
been called to exercise a ministry of care and responsibility in
this community. We pray for each one of them . . .

A minute's silence, or, if wished, all the names can be read out,
with a slight pause after each one.

Grant them wisdom, patience and the ability to listen to each
other and to the needs and desires of those they represent,
that through their dedication and hard work, this parish may
be duly cared for, and the life of all its people enhanced; thus
will the kingdom of God be brought nearer. **Amen.**

Members of the Parish Council sit down.

and/or

We pray for your blessing upon all who are citizens of this
place. Give your grace to those who occupy positions of
authority, that they may fulfil their responsibilities with
wisdom and equity and in the fear of God. Grant that true
faith, honest dealing and mutual service may be the standard
of our common life; and make us strong to meet every
challenge which the coming days may bring; through Jesus
Christ our Lord. **Amen.**

and/or

We lift up our hearts, O Lord, in intercession for all who carry
civic and political responsibilities. Grant that, putting aside all
merely selfish ambition, they may seek to be the instruments
of your will and carry out your purpose for the welfare of our
people; and may they both seek and see your glory in happier
human lives, through Jesus Christ our Lord. **Amen.**

(from Leslie Weatherhead, *A Private House of Prayer*)

Let us sum up all our prayers in the words of The Lord's Prayer.

The Lord's Prayer (page 227)

Blessing

May God the Creator,
God the Son
and God the Holy Spirit walk with you
and bless you in all that you do
all the days of your life. **Amen.**

Final Hymn

'I, the Lord of sea and sky' (HO&N 332)

Members of the Council follow the minister to the back of the
church. If they wish, either the leader or all members of the
Parish Council may shake the hands of those present.

Reading: The Vision of the Kingdom of God

The vision for wholeness and peace, which shines like a
beacon of light through the Old Testament, gives us important
insights into Christian simplicity. This theme is wonderfully
gathered up in the Hebrew word *shalom*, a full-bodied concept
that resonates with wholeness, unity, balance. Gathering in
(but much broader than) peace, it means a harmonious,
caring community with God at its centre as the prime sustainer
and most glorious inhabitant. This great vision of *shalom*
begins and ends our Bible. In the creation narrative, God
brought order and harmony out of chaos; in the Apocalypse of
John, we have the glorious wholeness of a new heaven and a

new earth. The messianic child to be born is to be Prince of Peace; justice and righteousness and peace are to characterise his unending kingdom (Isaiah 9.6, 7). Central to the dream of *shalom* is the wonderful vision of all nations streaming to the mountain of the temple of God to be taught his ways and to walk in his paths; to beat their swords into ploughshares and their spears into pruning hooks (Isaiah 2.2–5, Micah 4.1–4). *Shalom* even carries the idea of a harmonious unity in the natural order: the cow and the bear become friends, the lion and the lamb lie down together, and a little child leads them (Isaiah 11.6–7). We are in harmony with God – faithfulness and loyalty prevail. We are in harmony with our neighbour – justice and mercy abound. We are in harmony with nature – peace and unity reign.

Economically and socially, the vision of *shalom* is captured in what Bishop John Taylor calls 'The Theology of Enough'. The greed of the rich is tempered by the need of the poor. Justice, harmony, equilibrium prevail. 'It meant a dancing kind of inter-relationship, seeking something more free than equality, more generous than equity, the evershifting equipoise of a life-system'. Excessive extravagance, vaunting ambition, ravaging greed – all are foreign to the complete, contented brotherhood of *shalom*. Under the reign of God's *shalom*, the poor are no longer oppressed because covetousness no longer rules.

In a particularly tender scene, Jeremiah lamented the fraud and greed of prophet and priest, saying, 'They have healed the wound of my people lightly, saying "Peace, peace, when there is no peace"' (Jeremiah 6.14). In essence, Jeremiah had filed a malpractice suit against the self-styled religious quacks. They had put a Band-Aid over a gaping social wound and said 'Shalom, shalom – all will be well.' But Jeremiah thundered in effect '*En shalom* – all is not well. Justice is spurned, the poor oppressed, the orphan ignored. There is no wholeness or healing here!'

But the healing peace of God will not be spurned for ever. Isaiah saw a day when the reconciliation between people will be a reality; a day when justice and righteousness will reign, a time when the wholeness of God's peace will rule and people will 'walk in the light of the Lord' (Isaiah 2.4–5).

(From Richard J. Foster, *Freedom of Simplicity*)

Riders' Sunday

Background

Horseman's Sunday on Epsom Downs is a much-loved annual event which has been held every September since 1945. It gives hundreds of amateur riders from all walks of life the chance to gather at the home of one of the most famous horse races in the world. There is a simple ecumenical service in which those present give thanks for their horses and ponies and for those who support them. Following the service, there is a parade around part of the Derby course.

The service is taken by a minister on horseback. People on foot and drivers of carts or carriages are also invited to take part. Proceeds go to several charities, including the Riding for the Disabled Association and the Injured Jockeys Fund.

It may not be possible to visit Epsom but a service can be set up at a riding centre or farm for local riders and horse owners. A good alternative venue would be an equine sanctuary or rehabilitation centre.

Preparation

Decide whether the service should include horses and ponies led in hand and driving turnouts, as well as riders. If there are driving turnouts, then there should be two people with each; one person should stand at the horse's head during the service (as is normal practice at shows).

Post notices in local saddleries, feed merchants etc. and advertise the service in the local paper. Try to find a local music group, such as a brass group, to play beforehand and accompany the hymns.

A local feed merchant or saddlery might be asked to sponsor commemorative rosettes for the event. If possible, follow the service with a ride over the land, or a hack or pleasure drive along the roads.

If large numbers are expected to go on the road, contact the police, so that other traffic can be warned.

....

Welcome

We are here today because of our love of horses,
and our gratitude for all the enjoyment they give us.
Let us remember that our horses and ponies
are part of God's creation and precious to him;
and that one day we will have to account
for the way in which we have treated them.

Hymn

'All creatures of our God and King', verses 1 and 2 (HO&N 6)

Poem: The Horse

Where in this wide world can
man find nobility without pride,
friendship without envy or beauty
without vanity? Here, where
grace is laced with muscle, and
strength by gentleness confined.

He serves without servility; he has
fought without enmity. There is
nothing so powerful, nothing less
violent, there is nothing so quick,
nothing more patient.

England's past has been borne on
his back. All our history is his
industry; we are his heirs, he
our inheritance.
(Ronald Duncan, 1914–82)

Hymn

'All creatures of our God and King', verse 7

Reading (Job 39.19–25, NIV)

Do you give the horse his strength
or clothe his neck with a flowing mane?
Do you make him leap like a locust,
striking terror with his proud snorting?
He paws fiercely, rejoicing in his strength,
and he charges into the fray.
He laughs at fear, afraid of nothing;
he does not shy away from the sword.
The quiver rattles against his side,
along with the flashing spear and lance.
In frenzied excitement he eats up the ground;
he cannot stand still when the trumpet sounds.
At the blast of the trumpet he snorts, 'Aha!'
He catches the scent of battle from afar,
the shout of commanders and battle cry.

or

Poem: The Gift of Horses

Body speaks to body,
Mind to mind
And heart to heart.
What we know, he does not know but feels,
And this melds us into one, our horses and ourselves.

We minister through our tending and our training,
In thankfulness for all they give us.
They worship their creator in response,
Forever growing in confidence and beauty.
Sad the sight when God is neither Lord nor King –
They cringe and suffer,
They feel alone, turned in upon themselves
Or else lash out in pain at what torments them.

O God, grant that the horses in our care
May worship you and praise you through our loving;
Harsh it may seem at times,
Since hand or word or whip
Needs must control a marvellous creation

Of muscle, bone and brain,
Which uncontrolled can kill, or maim for ever.
As with a child,
Our love must set them limits
So that they know their rightful way of going.

A wondrous gift is this for all our race;
And yet we should remember
That it was not equine pride and pomp
That Jesus chose on his triumphal day,
But a humble ass, a sign of kingship come in peace.

(Noël Lovatt)

A short address or talk by leader or local horseman/woman

Prayer

O God, who created both the human race
and the creatures with whom we share the earth:
inspire us with reverence for your creation,
and help us to be fitting partners
for the horses and ponies in our care.
Bless those who work to relieve suffering
among horses in this and every land,
by spreading knowledge
and putting an end to abuse.
We ask this in the name of Jesus Christ
who died that all creation
might be reconciled to the One who made it. **Amen.**

or

God in heaven,
we thank you that we are privileged
to love and care for horses and ponies,
who give us so much in return.
Give us the wisdom to understand them
so that living together in concord
we may here be given a taste of heaven,
where at the last all beasts and humans
will live together in the glorious freedom
of the children of God. **Amen.**

Hymn

'Guide me, O thou great redeemer' (HO&N 252) *or*
'All things bright and beautiful', verses 1, 2, 3, 6 (HO&N 25)

(A collection can be taken for a local cause, or Riding for the
Disabled Association, International League for the Protection of
Horses, etc.)

Blessing of the Animals

My four-footed brothers and sisters,
large and small, young and old,
you who give so much to those who tend you:
may you be blessed in your stables
and blessed at your grazing.
May you be kept safe when you travel
and when you work in field and arena.
May you live in harmony
with your human friends all life long.
My sisters and brothers, the Lord bless you. **Amen.**

Blessing of the People

May our God, who made both human and beast,
bless you in your going out and your coming in.
May God bless you in your tending
and bless you in your riding [and driving].
And may God give you joy
in your companionship,
both today and in years to come. **Amen.**

or

The Grace

Let us say together:

**The grace of our Lord Jesus Christ,
and the love of God,
and the fellowship of the Holy Spirit,
be with us all evermore. Amen.**

Hand out any commemorative rosettes.

Additional prayers

These are suitable as part of a longer service without animals in an indoor riding arena or at an equine sanctuary. Use some small bales of straw for seating. You could have as a focal point a pile of bales covered with a cloth depicting horses and ponies. Choose those sections of the prayers that are appropriate for the occasion.

Let us give thanks for all those people and places
that make our lives as horse owners possible and fulfilling.

We give thanks and pray to God
for saddlers and harness makers,
saddleries and feed merchants,
and those who supply other necessaries;
remembering especially [*names of local suppliers*].
Give us thankful hearts.

We give thanks and pray to God
for instructors and trainers,
that they may instil confidence,
knowledge and the love of harmony;
remembering especially [*names of local instructors*].
Give us thankful hearts.

We give thanks and pray to God
for those who provide places for us
to keep and ride our horses:
owners of riding schools and trekking centres,
farmers and others who run livery yards;
remembering especially [*names of local owners of yards*].
Give us thankful hearts.

We give thanks and pray to God
for those who give up their time
to organize shows and competitions,
for the officers in riding and pony clubs;
remembering especially [*names of local officers and organizers*].
Give us thankful hearts.

We give thanks to God and pray
for all those who work to cure horses
that are damaged in mind or body:
vets and healers, equine hospitals and sanctuaries,
officers working to stop abuse;
remembering especially [*names of local vets, the RSPCA, etc.*].
Give us thankful hearts.

We give thanks and pray to God
for those running studs
to ensure the breeding of good horses,
for those who work to preserve native breeds
in danger of extinction;
remembering especially [*name of local stud or centre*].
Give us thankful hearts.

We give thanks and pray to God
for those who lovingly help disabled riders,
both those disabled in their bodies
and those whose minds are damaged or childlike;
remembering especially [*name of local RDA, etc.*].
Give us thankful hearts.

We give thanks and pray
for racing yards which give employment
and seek to bring their horses to perfection,
giving pleasure to owners and racegoers;
remembering especially [*name of local yard*].
Give us thankful hearts.

We give thanks and pray to God
for those individuals and organizations
that work to improve the lot of equines abroad,
horses, mules and donkeys,
which are essential to their owners' livelihood;
remembering especially [*name of charity being supported*].
Give us thankful hearts.

Let us sum up all our prayers in the words of
The Lord's Prayer.

The Lord's Prayer (page 227)

Thanksgiving for Water

Background

'Ho! Everyone who thirsts, come to the waters', says the opening of Isaiah 55, in his invitation to abundant life. Without water there can be no life, at least not in any form that we currently understand. From conception to the grave, water is within and without us. It is there in our daily lives and in our rituals: from that first ritual wash after birth, through baptism and use in many eucharistic services, to our final washing after death, water is an integral part of our lives. It sustains and cleanses us; it provides an avenue for leisure and transport. We use water in our language; we speak of it literally and metaphorically. There are well over a thousand references to it in the Bible. So let us give thanks to our Creator for this source of life.

Service at a well or spring

Responses

The Creator God turns a desert into pools of water:
a parched land into springs of water.
There the hungry live,
and they establish homes to dwell in.
They sow fields and plant crops,
and get a fruitful yield.
By the blessing of the Creator they multiply greatly.

Reading (Isaiah 41.17–20, NRSV)

When the poor and needy seek water, and there is none,
and their tongue is parched with thirst,
I the LORD will answer them,
I the God of Israel will not forsake them.
I will open rivers on the bare heights
and fountains in the midst of the valleys;

I will make the wilderness a pool of water
and the dry land springs of water.
I will put in the wilderness the cedar,
the acacia, the myrtle, and the olive;
I will set in the desert the cypress,
the plane and the pine together;
so that all may see and know,
all may consider and understand
that the hand of the LORD has done this,
the Holy One of Israel has created it.

Hymn

'Peace is flowing like a river' (HO&N 553)

Responses

In the beginning, the waters covered the land:
Cooling and cleansing.
Birthing waters of the earth:
Protecting and nourishing.
Mighty rivers and trickling streams:
Lifeblood of the land.
Crystal fountains and holy wells:
Sustaining our bodies and nourishing the earth.
Jesus said: 'Let anyone who is thirsty come to me.'
We believe! We will drink of Christ's living waters.
May our hearts and lives become
as rivers of living water to the world.
We will live lives that will nourish
and cherish God's creation.

Hymn: Let all who are thirsting

Let all who are thirsting
Come and drink of my waters
And you that have no money
Come and buy and come and eat.
Drink the life of the Spirit,
Drink of the living vine;
From the word of the Saviour
Spring the waters divine.

Let all who are seeking
Come and drink of my waters.
And you that are heartsore
Come and bathe in the stream. *Chorus*
Let all who are lonely
Come and drink of my waters.
And you that are sad and weary,
I will give you comfort and rest. *Chorus*

(Linda J. Probyn)

Tune: Afton Water; Scottish traditional

or 'Have you heard the raindrops' (HO&N 817)

Blessing

May the Spirit that moved over the waters cover you;
may Christ's living water sustain and nourish you;
may you and those you love
bathe in the light of God's love,
now and always.
And the blessing of the Triune God,
Creator, Preserver and Sustainer,
be with you and those you love, always. **Amen.**

or

The blessing of Almighty God be upon these and all waters;
springs and brooks, wells and lakes,
small and great rivers, and the great outer oceans.

The blessing of Almighty God be upon all ships and sailors,
on merchant seamen and fishermen,
and on all the brotherhood of the sea.

The blessing of Almighty God be with you all,
to lead you peacefully by still waters:
in the name of the Creator,
and of the Son
and of the Holy Spirit. **Amen.**

Reading at a place with flowing water (Psalm 78.15–16, NIV)

God split the rocks in the desert and gave the children of
Israel water as abundant as the seas; he brought streams out of
a rocky crag and made water flow down like rivers.

or (John 4.13, NIV)

Jesus said: 'Everyone who drinks this water will be thirsty again, but whoever drinks the water I give him will never thirst. Indeed, the water I give him will become in him a spring of water welling up to eternal life.'

History of well-dressing in Derbyshire

Well-dressing is something of a mystery. It was originally a pagan custom, to honour the spirit or nymph of the water source. Early Christians tried to put a stop to it. However, the tradition refused to die. Tissington revived well-dressing in 1349, as a thanksgiving for the village being spared a terrible outbreak of the Black Death that wiped out almost half the population of Britain. Baslow claims the villagers started dressing wells in Elizabethan times, but many places, including Youlgreave and Tideswell, began 'tap dressing' when piped water first came to town.

Well-dressing at its simplest is the art of decorating springs and wells with pictures made from growing things. Often dressers produce intricate and detailed pictures using only what nature provides. No two villages dress their wells in exactly the same way. A wooden tray is obtained, 6 feet high, 4 feet wide and over one inch deep. This is soaked in a local pond for a few days. Then it is hauled out and filled with soft wet clay. The artist brings the design, which is drawn full size on thin paper, and smooths it over the clay; then the work begins. Usually the dressers cut along each line of the picture with a sharp knife, then gently press small pieces of wood called 'barking' through the clay. Once the outline is finished, the picture is coloured in. In some villages this is called 'petalling' but in Holymoorside it is called 'flowering'. This is because they use whole flowerheads rather than individual petals.

Flowers are not the only thing that make up a well-dressing picture. Pumpkin seeds, cucumber leaves, acorns and even garlic skins have been used. Villages such as Foolow, which dress their wells later in the year, when there are fewer flowers, make good use of seeds and berries. Whatever method and materials are used, a well-dressing takes up to seven days of work by a whole team of people. It will then only last about a week before the clay dries and cracks and the flowers fade. Then it is taken down and the board stored away until the following year. Although some villagers carry out their work in secret, others invite people to watch as they dress the wells.

Although well-dressing is Derbyshire's most famous tradition, Chesterfield didn't take it up until 1864 when the pump in the Market Place was decorated after a very dry summer. The custom died out and wasn't revived until 1991, when only one well was decorated. This was in the Peacock Centre Courtyard on Low Pavement, and it was dressed in July as part of an exhibition about Derbyshire traditions. In 1992 the event spread around the town, with dressings on show at the Crooked Spire, the Central Methodist Church on Saltergate and Rose Hill United Reformed Church, as well as the Peacock Courtyard.

In Chesterfield the event is called the Blessing Parade and usually takes place during the second weekend in September. The Mayor leads the procession, followed by the Cock and Magpie and Garland dancers, with parishioners walking behind. Often the churches support different charities. The Central Methodist Church has emphasized the gift of water in other countries. Hymns are sung, coffee drunk and then the procession moves on to the next well.

This could be set up in any community. You do not need to have a genuine well to have a well-dressing. The communal feel will improve liaison between churches. Hymns, readings and prayers can be chosen to correspond with the theme of the well.

Well-dressing: children's activity

1. Talk to the children about well-dressing, its origin and use today.
2. Take the children out and select petals and flower heads.
3. Choose something simple as a theme, for example Noah and the ark and the rainbow.
4. Younger children can use glue and paper, using the petals to create a rainbow effect.
5. Older children can use clay on a wooden board with edges or frame. Using petals, seeds etc., they can either produce a rainbow or be more adventurous and create an ark.
6. These can be shown to the adults at the end of the service, with the children talking about the activity. A useful tip is to write the words on cards so that all the children can participate without feeling nervous.

Village Cricketers' Songs of Praise

Background

In many villages up and down the the country, cricket is still at the heart of the community. Although most teams now contain a mixture of local residents and those from farther afield, cricket provides a focus of commitment for a broad age-range of people who give of their time, effort and skills to help the local team be a source of pride. Pitches and outfields are lovingly cared for and pavilions are well maintained, not only for cricketing events but also often for a variety of social events. Adults put a lot of energy and thought into training young people, and many villages field excellent under-eighteen teams.

Many local women are responsible for the social life of the club, which can bring together a wide spectrum of age groups, and in some teams at least, women have been allowed to enter one of the last male bastions.

The village cricket club may be seen as a rival to the church, as a complement to the church, or even as an example of how the church could be if it were willing to involve all the players as actively as cricket does. It was indeed the sight of a cricket team in action which inspired Christopher Donaldson to write his penetrating prophecy about the future of rural ministry, *The New Springtime of the Church.*

A Cricketers' Service in which members of the team and supporters are encouraged to take part and to discover resonances between their regular activities and what the church has to offer can be a valuable bridge between these two focuses of community.

Preparation

There are usually members and/or supporters of the local cricket club who are also members of the local church. These are the people to approach first, unless they have already approached the church. Usually there are one or two members who are enthusiastic about the idea, and they can do the planning.

The first question is the venue, and possible ones are: a church building, the village hall, the pavilion, if large enough, and on the wicket. There are advantages and disadvantages with all four, but there is something to be said for bringing the cricketers into a church building for such an event.

Next, the choice of hymns. It is vital that they should be chosen by members of the club, so that they feel that it is their service and not something imposed on them. There are very few hymns directly relevant to cricket, perhaps only 'Fight the good fight', so it doesn't matter if the hymns bear little relation to the subject matter.

As this is a *Songs of Praise*-style service, the ideal is to set up interviews with as many as possible of those who choose the hymns. It is surprising how many people, including young ones, will respond to such a request, if given a bit of encouragement. Another alternative is to have three or four short testimonies from members on how they have been helped in their spiritual or general development by playing cricket. A third possibility is to have readings. There is a wealth of literature in praise of the virtues of cricket, and even some comparing cricket with the Christian life. Here are some examples:

Vita Lampada by Sir Henry Newbolt
A Cricketer's Pride by J. R. Thompson
'The Master Batsman' by Peter Gillot in *Cricket Writer*

It is also good to intersperse the service with pithy words of wisdom which in some way link cricket with faith. Suitable prayers are best made up for the occasion and read by players or supporters.

Suggestions for opening and closing the service are given below.

Welcome

I would like to welcome all of you here today.

In cricket, we are blessed with a most wonderful game which so reflects life. It is at one and the same time both about the individual and the team. The best captains, managers and selectors can handle each individual and get the very best out of them for the good of the team, provided that each member of the team believes in the captain, manager or selector.

And that is really where cricket and life meet. Our God is indeed the very, very best of captains, the very, very best of managers, the very, very best of selectors if we believe in him. With that belief, God will get the very best out of us individually and will make our congregation, our community and our world a rewarding, fulfilling and winning place in which to be.

Blessing

May the crease on which you bat always be smooth,
may the wind always carry the ball towards the boundary,
may you always have a good team to support you;
and may the blessing of God,
Father, Son and Holy Spirit,
be with you and with all those whom you love,
now and for ever. **Amen.**

Women's World
Day of Prayer

First Friday in March

The Women's World Day of Prayer is an important date in the calendar. For one day each year, Christian women from many traditions are united in prayer throughout the world. This occasion recognizes that most women live in rural settings and often do most of the agricultural work. It raises awareness of the plight of women world-wide and develops a bond in the love of Christ. The themes chosen usually highlight rural and financial difficulties experienced by women and their communities.

The international logo used by the Women's World Day of Prayer was designed by an Irish nun for the 1982 service. The cross is formed by stylized praying figures, their kneeling positions forming arrows coming together from the four corners of the earth. All are joined together within the circle of the world and enfolded in God's love.

Mary Ellen James, wife of a Presbyterian minister in Brooklyn, New York and mother of seven children, looked at the world around her and voiced her concern about the inhumane and poor quality of life she saw. Mary Ellen was aware of the problems faced by many women, particularly the new immigrants to America, including poverty, unemployment, poor housing and lack of health or educational facilities. In 1887 Mary Ellen called for a day to be set aside for prayers, 'where there shall be a confession of individual and national sins with offerings that fitly express the contrition.'

In 1891, two Baptist missionaries, appalled by the deprivation of women in other parts of the world, called for a day of prayer for overseas missions.

In 1919, the two separate days were united and the Women's World Day of Prayer came into being. The first service was held in Scotland in 1930, then in England in 1932, in Wales in 1933 and in Ireland in 1935. After the Second World War, the movement grew dramatically. By 1968, 127 countries were participating. It was decided that an international committee should be set up to undertake the work previously done by those in the United States of America. This international committee would include representatives of all national committees and would meet every four years.

At this meeting an international chairperson is elected and an international executive committee set up, with representatives from the eight regions of the world: Africa, Asia, the Caribbean, Europe, Latin America, North America, the Middle East and the Pacific.

At the international meetings, themes and writers for future years are chosen. These themes are then allocated to countries which have expressed a desire to prepare an order of service. Selection usually results in a wide geographical variation, such as Madagascar (1998), Venezuela (1999), and Indonesia (2000). The national committee of the chosen country prepares a draft order of service which they submit to the international executive.

The Day of Prayer starts on the International Date Line; the first service is held at dawn in Queen Salote's Girls' School in Tonga. Then, as the earth rotates, a great 'Mexican wave' of prayer sweeps through the Pacific and Asia, through countries like Fiji, New Zealand, Japan, the Philippines, Korea, Bangladesh and Africa; through the Middle East, Lebanon, Egypt and Cyprus to Europe; then West across the Atlantic to the Caribbean and South, Central and North America, till the last service of the day is held on an island off the coast of Alaska.

Through the Women's World Day of Prayer, women are encouraged:

- to become aware of the whole world and no longer live in isolation;
- to be enriched by the faith experience of Christians in other countries;
- to take up the burdens of other people and pray both with and for them;
- to become aware of their talents and use them in the service of society.

Prayer

O Lord, we thank you
that you made women in your own image,
to be both the guardians of life
and loving companions and helpers,
bearing with men the heat and burden of the day.
We pray for our sisters
in this country and throughout the world.
We pray that in fulfilling the tasks assigned to them,
they may be held in respect and honour,
and after journeying through this mortal life,
may reach at last the heavenly kingdom,
where you will wipe away the tears from every eye,
and unite us all in joy and gladness. **Amen.**

TIMES OF
TRAGEDY AND LOSS

At a Time of Crisis

Background

Farming has always been subject to good times and bad times.
The weather plays less of a dramatic part than it did in days gone
by, thanks to modern equipment and scientific knowledge.
However, we are all aware that disease can still ravage individual
farms or even national herds, and the uncertainty of farming
today can lead to tragedy. The following might be found of value
in difficult situations, where the Christian community can act as a
local focus and support.

Passage from the Psalms (see pages 223–6) *or*

Old Testament Reading (Habakkuk 3.17–18, NRSV)

> Though the fig tree does not blossom,
> and no fruit is on the vines;
> though the produce of the olive fails
> and the fields yield no food;
> though the flock is cut off from the fold
> and there is no herd in the stalls,
> yet I will rejoice in the LORD,
> I will exult in the God of my salvation.

> Lord, have mercy on your land and creatures.
> **Christ, have mercy on your human children.**
> Lord, have mercy on your whole creation.

New Testament Reading (from Romans 8, NRSV)

> What then are we to say about these things? If God is for us, who
> is against us? He who did not withhold his own Son, but gave him
> up for all of us, will he not with him also give us everything else?
> Who will separate us from the love of Christ? Will hardship, or
> distress, or persecution, or famine, or nakedness, or peril, or
> sword? I am convinced that neither death, nor life, nor angels,
> nor rulers, nor things present, nor things to come, nor powers,
> nor height, nor depth, nor anything else in all creation, will be
> able to separate us from the love of God in Christ Jesus our Lord.

Prayer for those in uncertainty and trouble

O Lord, in our lives
we are going through a time
of clambering over rocky outcrops
and drinking at turbulent, muddy streams.
Shadows are all about us
and we are fearful all the time.
Where are you, with your rod and staff?
Where is the comfort that you promise us?
Bring us safely through this time of trouble,
that our hunger and thirst may be satisfied,
that our fear may be calmed
and our souls restored.
Then shall we praise you,
walking in the paths of righteousness
and seeking to follow you all our days. **Amen.**

Responses

God is our refuge and strength,
an ever-present help in trouble.
Rejoice, the Lord is King!
Therefore we will not fear, though the earth give way
and the mountains fall into the heart of the sea.
Rejoice, the Lord is King!
He will bind up the broken-hearted
and release the oppressed.
Rejoice in the Lord, and again I say, Rejoice!
Do not be anxious,
but in everything
make your requests known to God.
Rejoice in the Lord, and again I say, Rejoice!
And the peace of God, which passes all understanding,
will keep your hearts and minds in Christ Jesus.
Thanks be to God.

Blessing

May the God of might and mercy,
who brought again our Lord Jesus
from the tomb into the glory of Easter Day,
raise you from the dust into new life.

May our Saviour, the sun of righteousness,
risen with healing in his wings,
shine upon you with his marvellous light.

May the Holy Spirit, the comforter,
be constantly by your side,
supporting and strengthening you
on the path you tread.

And may the Holy Trinity
guard, preserve and bless you
and all those whom you love,
now, and in the days to come. **Amen.**

Hymn at a time of crisis

A brighter dawn is breaking,
And earth with praise is waking;
For thou, O King most highest,
The power of death defiest;

And thou hast come victorious,
With risen body glorious,
Who now for ever livest,
And life abundant givest.

O free the world from blindness,
And fill the world with kindness,
Give sinners resurrection,
Bring striving to perfection;

In sickness give us healing,
In doubt thy clear revealing,
That praise to thee be given
In earth as in thy heaven.

(Bishop G. E. L. Cotton, 1813–66; LM; tune: New Sabbath)

Other suggested hymns

'Guide me, O thou great redeemer' (HO&N 252)
'Father, I place into your hands' (HO&N 162)
'In heavenly love abiding' (HO&N 323)
'O Love that will not let me go' (HO&N 517)

Good Friday 2001

Background

Disease and death are familiar companions to farmers and farming families, but every so often they come in an overwhelming form. The Great Cattle Plague of 1866 was such a disaster. This was not foot and mouth disease but rinderpest, a disease that causes death within days, wiping out herds and destroying livelihoods in a very short period. It was widespread enough for special prayers to be composed and said throughout the country. With no welfare state or system of compensation, many families were ruined.

The foot and mouth outbreak in 1967 is still vividly remembered by older people, and later in the twentieth century farmers were hit by salmonella scares, BSE and swine fever. However, nothing surpassed the horror of the foot and mouth epidemic in 2001. The following piece is suitable for private perusal, as a reading during a Good Friday three-hour service, or during a service for the loss of a complete herd. In May 2001 the Reverend Patricia Pinkerton wrote from the Forest of Dean:

> During the whole of the foot and mouth crisis, I have been in contact with the farming community and the NFU. Using a farmer six miles away, who knew all farmers in an eight-mile radius, and another equally on the other side of my area, I would pick up local farming data, and any changes ordered daily by MAFF. The information was swapped over to each area, added to by internet bulletins. Thus we were able to keep a large number of farmers informed very easily. I had always said that in a rural area, pastoral care comes in many forms, and that as a member of the clergy, I would stand by the side of any family that needed help during the crisis of foot and mouth. This was put to the test on Good Friday, Friday 13th April, 2001. On Maundy Thursday, a local farmer was told that because of 'contiguous cull', or ' likely dangerous contact'

from roaming forest sheep, his flocks and herds were to be slaughtered.

MAFF, the army (two soldiers, one on the gate, the other directing operations), five slaughterers, two MAFF observers and three vets were to descend on the farm the next day. On Good Friday (fortunately I had not been assigned to do any services), I arrived at the farm at approximately 10.30 a.m., wearing a clergy collar as requested by the family. They felt a need for the church to be present in their time of need. I was met at the farm gate by an army sergeant, who instructed me to disinfect my wellies (always kept in the car for rural visits) and to garb myself in an official white MAFF protective suit. I truly looked like Lazarus newly risen from the grave. Inside I felt less than alive. One hour later three MAFF vets arrived. One, the 'chief vet', had graduated from veterinary college in June 2000. He was to be assisted by two fifth-year vet students, who would take care of the injections for the animals, and also check all the stock visually for symptoms of foot and mouth disease. They were followed by a team of five professional slaughterers from the Berkeley Hunt, aged between 26 and 50. Each was garbed in the appropriate clothing, which was to be changed between the groups of animals slaughtered. There were two MAFF observers, also under 30 years of age.

The valuer then arrived to check the passports of each dairy cow, with name and ear tags, against the farmer's sheaves of paper, and they went down the yard to the farmhouse, for what turned out to be a seven-hour check of valuation levels. I was thankful the farmer was to be kept busy and away from the yard. I was quite sure that he had said his quiet farewells as he touched each cow, before departing to the house. The farmer's mother, amazingly strong, and remembering days past when she and her husband had farmed the land, recently bereaved, decided with difficulty not to go to the sheds for the slaughtering. I found myself in the next minutes offering to take her place, to ensure for her that every animal could be afforded its due dignity in death.

Thus on Friday 13th April, 2001, I came as close as I can ever remember to standing at the foot of the cross at Jesus's crucifixion: the army and slaughterers . . . the Roman soldiers; the two MAFF observers . . . Pilate's men; the vets and I . . . the three Marys; and the senior vet . . . the beloved disciple, standing there on that fateful day.

I stepped into the first shed, where all the ewes and lambs were penned, often ewe and lambs together. The lambs were gently picked up and held by the sons-in-law of the family, grim-faced and purposeful. I held the bottle of opiate called Euthanasia, for the vets to draw up the liquid into the syringe, to be plunged into the heart of each dear soul. I was so aware that I had in one pocket of my trousers a copy of the Twenty-third Psalm, and a cross in the other. I said quiet words of blessing, as the ewe watched her new offspring and then received the bolt in her head, an action repeated throughout the large flock, with the ram almost last. I felt he appeared to know that he must watch 'his flock until the last'. Every animal was again touched in death, and visually cleared of any signs of the disease.

Silently cups of tea and coffee were brought up the yard by a family member, to give a break and change of bloodied clothing before moving to the dairy herd, then heifers, followed lastly by the bull calves that had not gone to market. A touch on the shoulder by a dear friend came, followed by a hug of comfort, like the Peace, and this brought silent, wordless understanding.

The dairy cows seemed larger than life; hurdles were moved by whoever had free hands, to persuade the cows gently into the familiar and natural environment of the milking parlour. One by one they were gently injected with sedative before going back into the yard, and then the bolt. As each great milking beast fell to the ground, the silence grew louder; even the slaughterers were quiet – they were there to do a job, but with heavy hearts, for these animals were neither injured nor diseased. A true waste of life. Blood spurted onto the face of one of the slaughtermen, and he asked me to wipe it. Where was the crown of thorns, the vinegar and hyssop in this silent drama?

The heaviness of each beast as it hit the ground made me remember the readings in *Animals and Christianity* (ed. Andrew Linzey and Tom Regan). If God made this beast, then it would return to him. We moved slowly to the heifers, and then to the large barn with 34 bull calves. They were across the road, which necessitated extra disinfection. First the injection, then the bolt; the routine of it was incessant, and then came the pither who makes sure with his rod that the brainstem and nervous system were stilled. Blood, straw, muck, smell, silence, a quiet prayer and blessing, before returning to the farmstead. Was it already seven hours later, a pause in time, or the silence of eternity? All these animals were uninfected.

If anything could be humane this day, the longest ever, it was that it gave me the privilege of seeing a team of men and women doing a task as painful to them as was given to be necessary by the current MAFF orders. How important it will be for this farming family as they grieve to remember that for every Good Friday there is the promised Resurrection Day. I pray it will come to them soon.

Commemoration of the Death of an Animal

Background

Since earliest times, animals have played an integral part in the lives of humankind. First of all as a source of food, as sacrifices or as representatives of divine spirits, to be acknowledged or appeased; later as helpers in the hunt for food, controllers of vermin, guards of livestock, and companions in homes and places of work. Archaeology continues to reveal how great was the importance of animals in the lives of our ancestors.

Today

Much of this is still true. There is also increasing awareness of the important role that animals play in the rehabilitation of those in hospitals and care homes. We all know of the great benefits that are provided by guide dogs for the blind, hearing dogs for the deaf, search and rescue, riding for the disabled, etc. And for many in our society of dispersed families, animals may be their only companions.

Alongside all the benefits that humans derive from their relationship with the animal kingdom is the awareness that all of God's creatures need the same care and consideration as we demand for ourselves; that they also have the right to freedom from pain, hunger and thirst as we do, and that we have a duty to provide this. In short, when we take on the responsibility for an animal, that responsibility is ours for the lifetime of that animal, and it becomes an important part of our life and family.

To lose an animal that has been a companion and friend for many years can be a time of deep sorrow. For many people, where an animal has shared their home for many years, it can be a real trauma, equal to the death of a human friend or companion. As such it is right both to celebrate the times shared and to grieve for the loss that is experienced.

For many, the death of an animal will also involve considerable financial costs, especially if veterinary fees have to be met, so it is important to give careful consideration to this when planning how the body is to be dealt with. There are a number of alternatives, depending upon personal circumstances and preferences: pet crematoria and funeral services are available in many areas. If land is available in a garden or field, this may be the preferred option; then a decision has to be made about whether it is to be inhumation or cremation, and if cremation, are the ashes to be scattered or buried? Wherever possible it is a good idea to discuss these issues in advance so that hasty decisions do not have to be taken at the time of bereavement.

Opening Words (based on Psalm 104)

> How wonderful, O God, are your works.
> In wisdom you have made them all,
> and the earth is full of your creatures.
> You made provision for all their needs,
> you send forth your spirit
> and give life to all that lives;
> when the time is right,
> you take their breath away and they die.
>
> We have come together to say farewell to [*animal's name*] who has been a much-loved friend and companion to [*person's name*]. For a time they have walked together in their earthly journeys, sharing joy and sorrows in a spirit of comradeship and mutual respect.

Reading

> If I were alone in a desert and feeling afraid,
> I would want a child to be with me.
> For then my fear would disappear
> and I would be made strong.
> This is what life in itself can do
> because it is so noble, so full of pleasure
> and so powerful.
> But if I could not have a child with me
> I would like to have at least a living animal
> at my side to comfort me.

Therefore let those who bring about wonderful things
in their big dark books
take an animal to help them.
The life within the animal
will give them strength in turn.
For equality gives strength,
in all things and at all times.

(Meister Eckhart, 1290–1329)

Introduction

It is now time for [*animal's name*] to leave behind their earthly
journey, leaving [*person's name*] to grieve at her/his passing and
to mourn the empty space that has been left in her/his life.

[*Person's name*], we share your grief and mourn [*animal's
name*]'s passing.

This would be an appropriate place to inter the body or to scatter
or bury the ashes. A favourite piece of music could be played
quietly in the background during the actual burial or scattering.

[*Animal's name*], we give praise to God for your life
and we thank you for your faithfulness,
for your companionship, and for the joy
that you brought into [*person's name*]'s life.
We will remember you in our hearts.

If there has been an interment of the body or ashes, a plant, tree
or memorial can be planted or erected at this point if this is
possible. It is also a good place for a favourite poem, reading,
hymn or song.

Blessing

May God, the Creator of all, bless us.
May Jesus, the Redeemer of all, bless us.
May the Holy Spirit, the Sustainer of all, bless us.
May the Great Trinity bless us all,
present and departed,
now and always. Amen.

Stillbirth or Infant Death

Background

Facing and accepting the death of a loved one is almost always traumatic, even when that death is expected and comes at the end of a long and fulfilled life. When that death is sudden and involves someone whom we have thought of as just setting out upon their life journey, it inevitably brings to the fore a whole range of emotions and questions. It seems fair to say that one of the hardest things that any of us can be called upon to deal with is the death of a baby or young child and how to celebrate that life, whether it be a few hours or a few years. It also still happens that a baby is stillborn, either premature or full-term.

In our Western society, we have come a long way in pre-natal and perinatal care, and it therefore comes as a shock when things 'go wrong' and a baby dies in the womb or shortly after birth, and to some extent we have lost the ways of coping that our forebears had. Too often in the recent past, women and their families have been encouraged, no doubt with the best of intentions, to 'put it behind them', to forgo the essential grieving process, in some cases to the extent that some mothers and fathers have not even been able to see and hold their long-awaited baby. Thankfully, this is happening less and less, but there is still a dearth of resources available to help people to arrange a service for both celebrating and saying goodbye to the baby who has been such a large part of their life for those past few months. The following section offers ideas that can be used by families, clergy and others who may be asked to help with a service for a stillbirth or the death of a young child.

It is to be hoped that members of the wider family can be present on such an occasion, and perhaps some of them – grandparents, siblings, aunts or uncles – can participate by reading something or saying a few words of their own. This is something precious to hold on to through difficult times in the future. Needless to say, this will not always be possible or appropriate and pressure should never be brought to bear in such cases. It is also as well to be aware that whoever officiates, whether clergy or lay, may have the delicate task of coping with some fairly unusual requests at this time. It is important that those who are grieving should *not* be told that they cannot have this or do that; rather, they should be gently helped to find their own way to what is and is not possible.

Service 1

Opening sentences

To be conceived is to be chosen by God. No one is conceived or born by accident. Each life has a special destiny. Each person has a gift to give, a special task to perform, something that can be done by no one else. No matter how short a life has been, each one of us, every child of God, leaves an imprint on the world and on the lives of others.

There are no limitations of time and space upon the soul or upon love. There is a Divine Light which flows into and through the bonds of love which can never be severed or destroyed, and which even death itself cannot part. There is no cage for the soul. Love does not remain within the heart; it flows out to build secret temples in the landscape of the world.

Today we gather together to celebrate the gift that [*name*] brought to us, the gift of *her/his* life, and to give thanks for the love which *she/he* helped to grow in us. We come to say goodbye and give [*name*] into that eternal love which creates and enfolds all of life, in this world and the next.

There follows a hymn, song or other piece of music, during which a previously designated person may carry forward the casket in which the baby is to be interred to the minister or whoever is leading the service; at the same time the following prayer may be said, and an offering of the appropriate symbols may be made.

Prayer

[*Name*], three drops of water: a drop of your Creator, a drop of your Saviour, a drop of your Guardian Spirit; Holy Trinity of Love to bless and keep you on your journey to eternal life.

[*Parents' names*], a lighted candle to illumine the darkness in your time of grief.

[*Names of siblings, grandparents, etc.*], a rosebud to symbolize the potential of the future.

May the tender love of God be poured out upon you.
May the tender love of Christ enfold and comfort you.
May the tender love of the Holy Spirit fill you with peace.
May the encircling love of the Holy Trinity hold you in
    limitless love.
Now and for ever. **Amen.**

Readings

Either a religious passage or a favourite poem. Alternatively, a family member or friend may wish to say a few words.

[*Name*],
may the holy angels take charge of your beloved soul.
May they carry you tenderly to your new home,
to the loving God who holds out arms of purest light
to take you into his heart of love. **Amen.**

Blessing

On the days when the weight bows your back
and you stumble and fall, may the earth rise up
and dance to balance you.

In the time when the light dies in your eyes
and the ghosts of loss fill your heart,
may a rainbow come to you,
bathing you with colours of red, green, yellow and azure blue,
and may daisies and buttercups bring you a meadow of delight.

When the flood waters rise
and threaten to overwhelm you with darkness,
may the moonlight spread before you
a path of golden light to light your way.
May the wind of the Holy Spirit
blow over and around you,
wrapping you in a cloak of invisible power. **Amen.**

or

May God, who gave his Son to earth
that all might have life, bless you;
may God the Son, who bore our sins
and sorrows on the cross, bless you.

May God the Holy Spirit, who sustains
and strengthens all that lives, bless you;
And may the Holy Trinity surround you
and those dear to you with their love. **Amen.**

Service 2

Background

This is a memorial service, both for the recently bereaved and for those who lost babies or very young children years ago and have never been able to grieve for them.

Preparation

Provide some pens and a basket of loose flowers, each with a small card attached with space to write a child's name.

Place a table at the front with a large lighted candle and a sufficient number of smaller unlit candles for the expected numbers of people attending the service.

An appropriate piece of music should be played while the congregation is coming in.

Opening Sentence

On the third day he rose again from the dead, and ascended into heaven.

We have come here today to remember [*name*], and to acknowledge the special place that *she/he* holds in our hearts; to give thanks for the gift of [*name*]'s life, and for the special gifts that we have received by sharing in the time that *she/he* was a living presence with us.

Prayer

Holy Mary, Mother of God,
you knew the pain and suffering of losing a child.
You too had to stand by, helpless,
unable to do aught but weep.
You felt the sword of loss pierce your heart
and your soul was leaden.

Holy Mary, Blessed of God,
in the time of your darkest hour
you sought your child in his tomb
and found him gone.
Your tears fell like rain on the parched earth.

Holy Mary, Mother and Sister,
in the silence and fear of the upper room
your son came to you and to his friends,
he stood amongst you and said 'Peace be with you –
See, I am alive.'
You rejoiced that death could not hold him.
Death and the grave were conquered
by his dying and living.
And your heart leapt in hope.

Jesus: you are our hope in times of fear.
Jesus: you are our balm in times of pain.
Jesus: you are our joy in times of sorrow.
Jesus: you are the light in our darkness.
Jesus: you walk beside us in all our journeying.
Jesus: we welcome you in our midst.

At this point, it may be appropriate:

- for someone to say a few words about what it means to lose a child at birth or soon after birth;
- if there are only a few families present, for someone who shared in the preparations for the birth of a particular baby to say something about what the birth and loss means to them;
- to use one of the poems on pages 219–22.

Follow this with a favourite song, hymn or other piece of music and a short time of reflection.

Act of Remembrance

> Let us now remember these beloved children
> who shared our lives for a time
> and have now gone to a place of eternal light and life.

The leader reads out the names of those babies and children being remembered, while some gentle music is played very quietly in the background.

Members of the congregation are now invited to come forward. Those who have taken a flower place it in the bowl, speaking the name of the baby or babies whose lives they are remembering. Someone should be at the table to help with the lighting of the individual candles, which the congregation take back to their seats and take home with them if they wish. These candles can be lit again on what would have been the child's birthday as a sign of remembrance.

It is very important at this point in the service to allow sufficient time for everyone who wants to come forward, including those who are perhaps a little unsure until they gain confidence from those around them.

> God of tenderness, God of love,
> we give you thanks for the precious gift of these babies' lives.
> Though their lives on earth were too short a time for us,
> we know that their life with you is eternal.
> We know that, through the life and death of your Son, Jesus,

death has no power to separate us from you or from our loved
ones.
In this certain knowledge we give them into your loving care.
Grant them eternal peace, O Lord,
and may eternal light shine upon them.

Prayer of the Holy Spirit

O Lord our God, our souls trust in you;
hear my supplication and give heed to my prayer.
Elevate my spirit and give comfort to my heart.
Show me the light of your face.

Lord, for the sake of your mercy, support me
with the presence of your Spirit.

Lord, may your kingdom come,
may your justice be done,
may your truth prevail,
may your love be established,
and may you, Lord Jesus Christ,
the only-begotten Son of God,
dwell in your fullness within my soul.
And may the glory of the Lord God
be manifest in the Spirit of the Word
throughout all ages. **Amen.**

(Based on a prayer of Beinsa Douno (Peter Deunov, 1864–1944), from
Gems of Love)

Blessing

Vulnerable and loving God,
may your blessing come upon our spirits.
May our hearts and our souls be filled with your peace.
May our minds be filled with the knowledge of your loving
    compassion,
and may we go out from here firmly rooted in your presence,
resolved to follow in your footsteps
and to serve you in faith, love and joy.
In the name of the Christ,
Jesus our friend and Saviour. **Amen.**

Final Hymn

'Thine be the glory' (HO&N 672) (or hymn of own choice)

The flowers and cards which have been offered can be taken home or else taken up and placed upon the altar table, or on a table close to it, where they can remain throughout the week or until the flowers fade.

Poems

Paint My Life

Now take the sunshine from the sky
And the breezes passing by
And don't ask the reasons why,
Just paint my life.

Now take the autumn's misty chill
And a lonely windy hill,
Take a river running still
And paint my life.

Take the sound of horses' hooves,
Take the snow from cottage roofs,
Try, really try –
Let your mind touch clouds on high,
Just so long as you paint my life.

Take the beauty of a kiss,
Take the moments that you miss,
Take the magic of all this
And paint your life.

(Carolyn James in Harry Secombe, *The Second Highway Companion*)

Child of My Heart

You were the child of my heart –
Born of my womb
Blood of my blood
Bone of my bone.
Now you are gone from me
Too soon.
Tiny, fragile and precious
I held you
For that one and only time
Perfect in my eyes
I loved you.

The time which should have been a beginning
Became an end for me
As you slipped away from this world
To a place of light and
An even greater love than mine.
Through you, I was given a new understanding
A new love as
We shared our bond of life
I received the gift of joy,
Joy beyond measuring.
I felt you grow and live within my belly,
A living part of myself and
Yet separate
A life full of potential and possibilities.
I came to know how precious and how fragile life can be.

Tiny, fragile and precious
Your beauty lives in my heart
Alongside my love
A joy
A love
A beauty
That nothing can destroy
A bond that death cannot break.
A life that is a beginning.

(Linda J. Probyn)

Child of Our Love

Child of our love,
You have gone where we cannot follow you,
What you would have been,
What you would have done,
We cannot know.
There is farewell between us in this life,
A moving on through pain and grief and anger,
With loss ne'er finally accepted nor pain assuaged,
Until the days we tread the selfsame path.
In life to come, once more there'll be a meeting,
A holding out of arms and an embracing:
No more tears nor any separation,
But joy and union, in God's marvellous light.
Beloved one, we cannot hold you in our arms,
But 'til that time we'll hold you in our hearts.

(Noël Lovatt)

Lullaby

This lullaby we sing for you,
Our dearest child, who never grew
From a soft flowering in the womb,
Your living home, your weeping tomb.

We'll never hold you in our arms,
Nor share your joys, nor soothe your harms;
But your flesh, blind to our day's light,
We trust to resurrection sight.

Your spirit, small one, has returned
To God the Father, whose love yearned
For you before eternity,
This tender glory you now see.

This lullaby we sing for you,
Our dearest child, with angels who
Delighting in the sabbath rest
Rejoice you wake on Jesus' breast.

(G. H. R., 1985)

A Blessing of the Western Highlands and Islands (adapted)

The lovely likeness of the Lord
Is in your pure face,
The loveliest likeness that
Was upon earth.

You are the joy of all joyous things,
You are the light of the sun,
You are the door of the chief of hospitality,
You are the the surpassing star of guidance,

You are the step of the deer of the hill,
You are the step of the steed of the plain,
You are the grace of the swan of swimming,
You are the loveliness of all lovely desires.

The best hour of the day be thine,
The best day of the week be thine,
The best in the Son of God's domain be thine.
Myriel and Mary Virgin has come,
Uriel* the all-beneficent has come,
Gabriel the seer of the Virgin has come,
Raphael the prince of the valiant has come,
And Michael the chief of the host has come,
And Jesus Christ the mild has come,
And the Spirit of true guidance has come,
And the King of kings has come on the helm,
To bestow on thee their affection and their love.

There are also suitable poems in *Rainbows through the Rain* by
Fiona Castle (widow of Roy Castle).

---

* Uriel is mentioned as the fourth archangel in Jewish apocryphal writings.

Passages from the Psalms

Background

The book of Psalms in our Bibles is a compilation of different collections of psalms written at various dates from the time of David onwards. It assumed its present form after the exile.

The psalms cover a wide range of human situations from desolation to triumph. Often the writer is not afraid to talk to God in tones of deep emotion, including reproach, anger and despair. The psalms are therefore writings that can help us to express difficult emotions in a time of crisis or tragedy. The following passages can be used in public or private. They all contain an even number of lines, so that they can be said responsorially, and this is how they are set out. The ones set out in groups of two or four lines can of course be said line and line about. All these passages are from the Revised English Bible.

Psalm 6

Show favour to me, LORD, for my strength fails;
LORD, heal me for my body is racked with pain;
I am utterly distraught.
When will you act, LORD?
Return, LORD, deliver me;
save me, for your love is steadfast.
I am wearied with my moaning;
all night long I drench my bed with weeping.
The LORD has heard my entreaty;
the LORD will accept my prayer.

Psalm 13

How long, LORD, will you leave me forgotten,
how long hide your face from me?
How long must I suffer anguish in my soul,
grief in my heart day after day?
Look, LORD my God, and answer me.
Give light to my eyes lest I sleep the sleep of death.
My heart will rejoice when I am brought to safety.
I shall sing to the LORD, for he has granted all my desire.

Psalm 27

The LORD is my light and my salvation;
whom should I fear?
The LORD is the stronghold of my life;
of whom then should I go in dread?
Hear, LORD, when I cry aloud;
show me favour and answer me.
'Come,' my heart has said, 'seek his presence.'
I seek your presence, LORD; hide not your face from me.
Well I know that I shall see
the goodness of the LORD in the land of the living.
Wait for the LORD; be strong and brave,
and put your hope in the LORD.

Psalm 28

To you, LORD, I call;
my Rock, do not be deaf to my cry,
lest, if you answer me with silence,
I become like those who go down to the abyss.
Blessed be the LORD,
for he has heard my voice as I plead for mercy.
The LORD is my strength and my shield,
in him my heart trusts.
I am sustained, and my heart leaps for joy,
and with my song I praise him.
Save your people and bless those who belong to you,
shepherd them and carry them for ever.

Psalm 44

Rouse yourself, LORD; why do you sleep?
Awake! Do not reject us for ever.
Why do you hide your face,
heedless of our misery and our sufferings?
For we sink down to the dust
and lie prone on the ground.
Arise and come to our aid;
for your love's sake deliver us.

Psalm 69

Save me, God,
for the water has risen to my neck.
I sink in muddy depths
where there is no foothold;
I have come into deep water,
and the flood sweeps me away.
I am exhausted with crying,
my throat is sore,
my eyes are worn out
with waiting for God.
At an acceptable time
I lift my prayer to you, LORD.
In your great and enduring love,
answer me, God, with sure deliverance.
Rescue me from the mire,
do not let me sink.
I am afflicted and in pain;
let your saving power, O God, set me securely on high.
I shall praise God's name in song
and glorify him with thanksgiving.

Psalm 143

LORD, hear my prayer; listen to my plea;
in your faithfulness and righteousness answer me.
An enemy has crushed me underfoot,
and left me to lie in darkness like those long dead.

My spirit fails me and my heart is numb with despair.
I call to mind times long past;
I think over all you have done;
the wonders of creation fill my mind.
Athirst for you like thirsty land,
I lift my outspread hands to you;
Do not hide your face from me
or I shall be like those who go down to the abyss.
In the morning let me know of your love,
for I put my trust in you.
Show me the way that I must take,
for my heart is set on you.
Revive me, LORD, for the honour of your name;
be my deliverer; release me from distress.
In your love for me, destroy my enemies,
for I am your servant.

Appendix 1:
The Lord's Prayer

Our Father in heaven,   *or*   Our Father, which art in heaven;
hallowed be your name,   hallowed be thy name.
your kingdom come,   Thy kingdom come.
your will be done,   Thy will be done,
on earth as in heaven.   in earth as it is in heaven.
Give us today our daily bread.   Give us this day our daily bread.
Forgive us our sins, as we forgive   And forgive us our trespasses,
   those who sin against us.   as we forgive them that
Lead us not into temptation   trespass against us.
but deliver us from evil.   And lead us not into temptation,
For the kingdom, the power   but deliver us from evil.
and the glory are yours,   For thine is the kingdom,
now and for ever. Amen.   the power, and the glory,
                                                  for ever and ever. Amen.

(from *Common Worship*)   (from the Book of Common Prayer)

On occasions the following version may be seen as appropriate:

ETERNAL Spirit,
Life-Giver, Pain-Bearer, Love-Maker,
Source of all that is and that shall be,
Father and Mother of us all,
Loving God, in whom is heaven:

May the Hallowing of your Name echo through the universe.
The Way of your Justice be followed by the peoples of the world.
Your Heavenly Will be done by all created beings.
Your Commonwealth of Peace and Freedom sustain our hope and
     come on earth.
With the bread we need for today, feed us.
In the hurts we absorb from one another, forgive us.
In times of temptation and test, strengthen us.
From trials too great to endure, spare us.
From the grip of all that is evil, free us.

For you reign in the glory of the power that is love,
now and for ever. Amen.

(from Jim Cotter, *Prayer at Night*)

Appendix 2: Christian Rural Organizations

Agricultural Christian Fellowship (ACF)
ACF celebrates a down-to-earth God for a down-to-earth profession. It links students, farmers and others in agriculture in witness to Christ. ACF founded Farm Crisis Network, jointly with the Arthur Rank Centre. It collaborates with the Church Mission Society and the John Ray Initiative 'Agriculture and Theology Project'. ACF organizes conferences and local groups, and publishes a newsletter.

Contact details:
Dr Peter Carruthers, Chairman, Agricultural Christian Fellowship, UCCF, 38 De Montfort Street, Leicester LE1 7GP
Tel: 0116 255 0362
E-mail: <acf@uccf.org.uk>
Web site: <www.agriculturalchristianfellowship.org.uk>

Arthur Rank Centre
Situated at the National Agricultural Centre (NAC) near Coventry, the Arthur Rank Centre is recognized as the national rural resources unit for the churches. It supports a range of initiatives to improve rural quality of life, especially for the disadvantaged, vulnerable and excluded. The Director is the Revd Dr Gordon Gatward.

Contact details:
The Arthur Rank Centre, Stoneleigh Park, NAC, Warwickshire CV8 2LZ
Tel: 024 7669 6969
E-mail: <arthur.rank.centre@virgin.net>
Web site: <arthurrankcentre.org.uk>. The contact details for a variety of rural organizations can be found at this web site.

Central Council of Church Bell Ringers

The Central Council and its affiliated societies world wide aim to promote the ringing of church bells and to represent the ringing exercise to the world at large. The Council provides expert advice and information to ringers, church authorities and the general public on all matters relating to bells and bell ringing.

Contact details:
Mr Ian Oram, Secretary, The Cottage, School Hill, Warnham, Horsham RH12 3QN
Tel: 01403 269743
E-mail: <ihoram@hotmail.com>
Web site: <www.ringingworld.co.uk>

Christian Ecology Link (CEL)

CEL seeks to create awareness of ecological problems and suggest responses. It also aims to create Christian understanding within the Green Movement.
CEL produces information leaflets and worship material.

Contact details:
Laura Deacon, Correspondent, Christian Ecology Link, 3 Bond Street, Lancaster LA1 3ER
Tel: 01524 33858
E-mail: <info@christian-ecology.org.uk>
Web site: <www.christian-ecology.org.uk>

Christian Rural Concern

Members of CRuC are committed to spreading a Christian understanding of rural and environmental issues. CRuC encourages, in the light of the gospel, an awareness of what is happening in rural areas and equips people to discover this through a course of study, essays and projects in association with the University of Keele.

Contact details:
Joy Gadsby, Secretary of CRuC, 5 Cedar Court, Addington Road, Sanderstead, South Croydon CR2 8RA
Tel: 020 8657 0831
E-mail: <joygadsby@sandersteadprsh.nildram.co.uk>
Web site: <www.cruc.org.uk>

John Ray Initiative (JRI)

JRI is an educational charity bringing together scientific and Christian understandings of the environment in a way that can be widely communicated and lead to effective action.

The Chairman is Sir John Houghton CBE, FRS and the Executive Director is Dr Peter Carruthers.

Contact details:
The John Ray Initiative, University of Gloucestershire, QW212, Close Hall, Swindon Road, Cheltenham GL50 4AZ
Tel: 01242 543580
E-mail: <jri@glos.ac.uk>
Web site: <www.jri.org.uk>

Rural Sunrise

Rural Sunrise is an ecumenical rural consultancy dedicated to enabling and encouraging rural churches as agents of God's mission, and helping individual churches to tailor a mission strategy appropriate to the local situation. It organizes conferences and publishes and distributes a range of resources for evangelism and teaching in rural communities. The Director is the Revd Barry Osborne.

Contact details:
2 Old Forge, Gardner Street, Herstmonceux, Hailsham,
East Sussex BN27 4NZ
Tel/fax: 01323 832445
E-mail: <sunrise@ruralmissions.org.uk>
Web site: <www.users.zetnet.co.uk/bosborne/sunrise.htm>

Rural Theology Association (RTA)

The aims of the RTA are to study the gospel and develop theology in a rural setting to raise awareness of the nature of rural ministry and worship, and to discover ways of living in the countryside that embody a Christian response to the world. RTA runs a major conference every two or three years, produces the journal *Rural Theology* and encourages the growth of local groups. Jane Hald chairs the executive committee.

Contact details:
Jane Hald, RTA Executive, 39 Prior's Acre, Boxgrove, Chichester,
West Sussex PO18 0ER
Tel: 01243 780044
Fax: 01243 788346
E-mail: <jane.hald@virgin.net>
Web page: <www.rural-theology.org.uk>

St Michael's (Princetown) Trust

This trust was set up in 1999 and aims to encourage, both within
and beyond the Christian Church, greater awareness of
environmental issues and our responsibility to care for the earth.
It organizes events, quiet days and short courses, and seeks to
develop liturgy inspired by the moorland setting and that is
relevant to present-day concerns.

Contact details:
St Michael's Trust Secretary, 1 Albert Terrace, Two Bridges Road,
Princetown, Devon PL20 6QP
Tel/fax: 01822 890412
E-mail: <stmpp@aol.com>
Web site: <users.daelnet.co.uk/allinson/cel/smpt.htm>

References, Sources and Copyright Acknowledgements

The authors and publisher also gratefully acknowledge permission to reproduce copyright material. Every effort has been made to trace and acknowledge copyright holders. The publisher apologizes for any errors or omissions that may remain and, if notified, will ensure that full acknowledgements are made in a subsequent edition of this book.

The Bible

Extracts have been taken from the following versions of the Bible:

The Authorized Version (AV) of the Bible (the King James Bible), the rights of which are invested in the Crown. Reproduced by permission of the Crown's Patentee, Cambridge University Press.

The HOLY BIBLE, NEW INTERNATIONAL VERSION (NIV) Copyright © 1973, 1978, 1984 by International Bible Society. Used by permission of Hodder & Stoughton Ltd, a member of Hodder Headline Plc Group.

The New Revised Standard Version (NRSV) of the Bible, copyright © 1989 by the Division of Christian Education of the National Council of Churches of Christ in the USA. Used by permission. All rights reserved.

The Revised English Bible (REB), copyright © Oxford University Press and Cambridge University Press, 1989.

The Revised Standard Version (RSV) of the Bible, copyright © 1946, 1952 and 1971 by the Division of the Christian Education of the National Council of Churches of Christ in the USA. Used by permission. All rights reserved.

The Book of Common Prayer

Extracts from The Book of Common Prayer, the rights in which are vested in the Crown, are reproduced by permission of the Crown's Patentee, Cambridge University Press.

Common Worship

Extracts from *Common Worship: Services and Prayers for the Church of England* are copyright © The Archbishops' Council, 2000 and are reproduced by permission.

General references

Allen, James, extract from *As a Man Thinketh*, Fleming H. Revell & Co, quoted in Reuben P. Job and Norman Shawchuck, *A Guide to Prayer for Ministers and Other Servants*, Nashville, TN: Upper Room 1983.

'A Children's Talk', in 'CEL Harvest Festival' reproduced by permission of Christian Ecology Link.

Adam, David, 'The shield of the Father' and 'Open the gate of Glory' from *Tides and Seasons: Modern prayers in the Celtic tradition*, SPCK 1989. Reproduced by kind permission of the author.

Adam, David, 'The Creator who brought order out of chaos' from *The Open Gate: Celtic prayers for growing spiritually*, SPCK 1994. Reproduced by kind permission of the author.

Bell, John L., 'When the time was right' from *He Was in the World*, Wild Goose Publications 1994. © WGRG, Iona Community.

Betjeman, John, 'Advent 1955', *Collected Poems*, John Murray 1989. Reproduced by permission of John Murray Ltd.

Blake, William, 'The Lamb', in John Simpson (ed.), *The Poetical Works of William Blake*, Oxford University Press 1956.

Blythe, Ronald, *Akenfield*, Penguin 1999.

Bunyan, John, *Pilgrim's Progress*, Collins 1953.

Castle, Fiona (ed.), *Rainbows through the Rain*, Hodder & Stoughton 1998.

Clare, John, 'The Setting Sun' in J. W. Tibble and Anne Tibble (eds), *Selected Poems*, Dent 1973.

Cotter, Jim, a version of the Lord's Prayer, *Prayer at Night*, Cairns Publications 1983; *Prayer at Night's Approaching*, Cairns Publications 2001. (A version of this prayer also appeared in *A New Zealand Prayer Book*, Collins 1989.) Reproduced by kind permission of the author.

Cummings, E. E., 'i am a little church' is reprinted from *Complete Poems 1904–1962*, edited by George J. Firmage, by permission of W. W. Norton & Company. Copyright © 1991 by the Trustees for E. E. Cummings Trust and George James Firmage.

Douno, Beinsa, *Gems of Wisdom and Love: Prayers and Formulas*, The Grain of Wheat Trust 1994.

Duncan, Ronald, 'The Horse', copyright © Ronald Duncan Foundation, in Miranda Weston-Smith (ed.), *Collected Poems*, Heinemann/Quixote Press 1981.

Eaton, John, *The Circle of Creation*, SCM Press 1995.

Eckersley, Glennyce S., extract from *Children and Angels* published by Rider 1999. Used by permission of The Random House Group Limited.

Foster, Richard J., *Freedom of Simplicity*, HarperCollins 1998.

Gasztold, Carmen Bernos de, *Prayers from the Ark*, trans. Rumer Godden, Penguin 1992.

George, James, *Asking for the Earth*, Element Books 1995.

Gibran, Khalil, *The Prophet*, Heinemann 1972.

'Glory to God', extract from the *Methodist Covenant Service*, Methodist Publishing House, reproduced with permission. Copyright is controlled by Trustees for Methodist Church Purposes.

Grahame, Kenneth, 'The Piper at the Gates of Dawn' from *The Wind in the Willows*, in Mervyn Wilson, *The Rural Spirit: Language of the earth and sky*, Collins 1990.

Hale, R. B., *The Beloved St Mungo Founder of Glasgow*, University of Ottawa Press 1989.

Hardy, Thomas, 'The Oxen', in *Collected Poems of Thomas Hardy*, Macmillan & Co. 1928.

Henken, E. R., *Traditions of Welsh Saints*, D. S. Brewer 1987.

Hildegard of Bingen, extract from Matthew Fox, *Original Blessing*, Santa Fe, CA: Bear & Co 1983.

James, Carolyn, 'Paint My Life' in Harry Secombe, *The Second Highway Companion*, Robson Books 1990.

Kipling, Rudyard, 'Eddi's Service (AD 687)', in *Rudyard Kipling's Verse: Inclusive Edition*, 1885–1932, Dent 1998. Reproduced by permission of A. P. Watt on behalf of The National Trust for Places of Historical Interest or Natural Beauty.

Kipling, Rudyard, extract from 'The Glory of the Garden', in *The Nation's Favourite Poems*, BBC Books 1998. Reproduced by permission of A. P. Watt on behalf of The National Trust for Places of Historical Interest or Natural Beauty.

Linzey, Andrew and Regan, Tom, *Animals and Christianity*, SPCK 1989.

MacCaig, Norman, 'In Praise of Collie' from *Collected Poems* published by Chatto & Windus 1985. Used by permission of The Random House Group Limited.

Rossetti, Christina, 'Consider the Lilies of the Field', *Complete Poems*, Penguin 2001.

Schweitzer, Albert, 'A Tree' in Erica Anderson, *The Schweitzer Album*, A & C Black 1965, p. 44.

Simpson, Ray, 'Trinity Triads' from *Celtic Worship Through the Year*, Hodder & Stoughton 1997, copyright © Community of Aidan and Hilda, is reproduced with the author's permission.

Ward, Wilf, 'We Like Sheep' and 'Wild Flowers' are reproduced by kind permission of the author.

Weatherhead, Leslie, *A Private House of Prayer*, Hodder & Stoughton 1958, copyright is controlled by Trustees for Methodist Church Purposes.

Wordsworth, William, 'To a Skylark' in Stewart Beer, *An Exaltation of Skylarks*, SMH Books 1995.

General hymn references

There is such a galaxy of hymn books that it is impossible to list all the books that have some relevant hymns. Each denomination has its own traditional books and updated versions. There are some collections which do not belong to any particular denomination but which have a good number of suitable hymns, and most references are to these books.

Hymns Old and New (HO&N). This refers to the Complete Anglican Version published by Kevin Mayhew in 2000. The music edition is ISBN 1840035668.

Common Ground (CG) calls itself 'A Song Book for all the Churches' and was published by St Andrew Press in 1998. Although there is a special emphasis on Scottish hymns it includes contributions from around the world. The music edition is ISBN 0715207539.

Mission Praise (MP) is updated and expanded frequently. The *Complete Mission Praise* was published by Marshall Pickering in 1999 (full music edition ISBN 0551040289; words edition ISBN 0551040270).

The Oxford Book of Carols (OB) was published in 1984 and is still in print in paperback (ISBN 01935331534).

Songs from Denmark is Lutheran and contains several songs which bring together Christian theology and appreciation of the natural world in a unique way. It is published by the Danish Cultural Institute. The second printing was in 1992 (ISBN 8777831837).

Other collections we have referred to include:

- *Come and Praise* (CP), published by BBC Consumer Publishing in 2000)ISBN 1853112658)
- *Junior Praise* (JP), published by Marshall Pickering in 1997 (combined music edition ISBN 0551026383)
- *English Hymnal*, published by Oxford University Press in 1933
- *New English Hymnal* (NEH), published by Canterbury Press Norwich in 1986 (full music edition ISBN 0907547516)

Many of the hymns suggested appear in hymn books in common use today. But in case there is difficulty in finding a hymn, we give its number in HO&N. If it is not present there, we give its number in other hymn books, or otherwise print it in full.

Specific hymn references

Curd, Jean, 'Ringing Through the Year', reproduced by kind permission of the author.

Fraser, Ian M., 'Lord, bring the day to pass', copyright © 1969 Stainer & Bell Ltd.

Grundtvig, N. F. S., 'Like the sunrise on the purple skies', in *Songs from Denmark*, Danish Cultural Institute 1992. Reproduced by kind permission of the Danish Cultural Institute.

Ingleby, Tony, 'Thank you, Father, for your care', copyright © 2000 Tony Ingleby, reproduced by kind permission of the author.

Low, Frank, 'We plough the fields with tractors', reproduced by kind permission of the author.

Masefield, John, 'O Christ who holds the open gate', in D. L. Couper (ed.), *Country Services*, Farmer & Stock-breeder Publications Ltd 1947. Reproduced by permission of the Society of Authors as the Literary Representative of the Estate of John Masefield.

Walling, Armorel K., 'Go tell all creatures in the world', in Tom Regan and Andrew Linzey (eds), *Song of Creation*, Marshall Pickering 1988. Reproduced by kind permission of the author.

Wren, Brian A., 'Thank you, God, for water, soil and air', copyright © 1975 Hope Publishing Company for the USA, Canada, Australia and New Zealand, and Stainer & Bell for all other territories.

Personal contributions

The authors would also like to thank all those who have contributed material for *Seasonal Worship from the Countryside*:

Mrs Elisabeth Ashworth for 'Christmas tree festival' on p. 3.

Mr Peter Atkinson for the background to 'Clypping Service' on pp. 40–1.

Dr Winifred Kingsbury for sending the poem 'Advent 1955' by Sir John Betjeman on pp. 5–6 and for 'Preparation of Harvest Festival on a farm' on p. 123.

The Revd Jonathan Lumby for a substantial contribution to 'Palm Sunday' on pp. 48–9.

The Revd Patricia E. Pinkerton for 'Good Friday 2001' on pp. 205–8.

'G. H. R.' for 'Lullaby' on pp. 221–2.

St Michael's (Princetown) Trust for 'Moorland Evening Worship' on p. 167.

The Revd Elfrida Savigear for the 'Procession of witness' on pp. 53–5.

The Revd Mark Turner for supplying an original version of the Clypping Service.